## TAX AND CULTURE

Tax scholars traditionally emphasize economics and assume that all tax systems can be evaluated in more or less the same way. By applying the insights of anthropology, sociology, and other social sciences, Michael A. Livingston demonstrates that tax systems frequently pursue different values and that the convergence of tax systems is frequently overstated. In *Tax and Culture*, he applies these insights to specific countries, such as China and India, and specific tax issues, including progressivity, tax avoidance, and the emerging area of environmental taxation. Livingston concludes that the concept of a global tax culture is, in many cases, merely a reflection of Western hegemony, and is unlikely to survive the changes implicit in the rise of non-Western nations and cultures.

Michael A. Livingston is Professor of Law at Rutgers Law School. He has been teaching tax and comparative law for thirty years and has published numerous articles on these subjects. His article "Reinventing Tax Scholarship" has been cited as an inspiration by various tax scholars.

# Tax and Culture

## CONVERGENCE, DIVERGENCE, AND THE FUTURE OF TAX LAW

MICHAEL A. LIVINGSTON
Rutgers University School of Law

CAMBRIDGE
UNIVERSITY PRESS

**CAMBRIDGE**
**UNIVERSITY PRESS**

University Printing House, Cambridge CB2 8BS, United Kingdom

One Liberty Plaza, 20th Floor, New York, NY 10006, USA

477 Williamstown Road, Port Melbourne, VIC 3207, Australia

314–321, 3rd Floor, Plot 3, Splendor Forum, Jasola District Centre, New Delhi – 110025, India

79 Anson Road, #06–04/06, Singapore 079906

Cambridge University Press is part of the University of Cambridge.

It furthers the University's mission by disseminating knowledge in the pursuit of education, learning, and research at the highest international levels of excellence.

www.cambridge.org
Information on this title: www.cambridge.org/9781107136847
DOI: 10.1017/9781316480144



First published 2020

*A catalogue record for this publication is available from the British Library.*

*Library of Congress Cataloging-in-Publication Data*
NAMES: Livingston, Michael A., author.
TITLE: Tax and culture : convergence, divergence, and the future of tax law / Michael A. Livingston.
DESCRIPTION: New York : Cambridge University Press, 2020. | Includes bibliographical references and index.
IDENTIFIERS: LCCN 2019043864 (print) | LCCN 2019043865 (ebook) | ISBN 9781107136847 (hardback) | ISBN 9781316480144 (ebook)
SUBJECTS: LCSH: Taxation – Law and legislation. | Taxation – Social aspects. | Fiscal policy.
CLASSIFICATION: LCC K4460 .L58 2020 (print) | LCC K4460 (ebook) | DDC 343.04–dc23
LC record available at https://lccn.loc.gov/2019043864
LC ebook record available at https://lccn.loc.gov/2019043865

ISBN 978-1-107-13684-7 Hardback

# Contents

# Acknowledgments

This book is the product of several years of work. Thanks are due to the Rutgers Law School for various means of supporting my research and to Arabelis Brito for outstanding research assistance. I wish also to thank my wife, Anne Weiss, for her support throughout the process, in particular for tolerating many long and only sometimes productive research trips. Finally, although they are too many to name, I wish to thank the many foreign tax scholars, officials, and others who helped me conduct the research for this book: without them, it would not have been possible.

I hope that the book contributes to a greater understanding of tax culture, and therefore to a more peaceful world.

# 1

# Introduction: Comparative Law and Its Relevance to the Tax Field

That law both affects and is affected by the surrounding culture is a proposition so obvious as to hardly need mentioning. Yet the precise direction and nature of this relationship is among the most vexing problems in comparative (or any) law. Is law a reflection of the surrounding culture or one of its principal constitutive elements? Do countries have a legal culture, or subculture, that is distinct from their more general cultural tendencies or is this a contradiction in terms? What does culture consist of in the first place: is it primarily a question of attitudes, institutions, or some combination of the two, and which of these is likely to be more important in a legal context? Are countries becoming more similar in their legal and nonlegal cultures – the so-called globalization phenomenon – or is this merely a comforting myth? Is the term "culture" itself of any real value, or is it so prone to generalization and misstatement as to do more harm than good?

The question of law and culture is particularly beguiling in a tax context. Of all areas of law, tax has perhaps the strongest claim to universality. All governments impose taxes, and – rhetoric aside – there is no country in which people do not prefer to pay fewer rather than more of them. The basic kinds of taxation – income, excise, property, etc. – are the same in all countries, and the essential vocabulary of tax policy (equity, efficiency, simplicity) is the same in every language. Yet it is obvious to even a casual observer that tax outcomes vary enormously between countries, even when they are at a similar economic level and impose superficially similar taxes. More sophisticated observers frequently observe that the "tax culture" or (more colloquially) the "tax system" of these countries is different in various ways. But the precise meaning of this term is often indeterminate, and the relationship of a country's tax culture to its broader legal (or general) attitudes and institutions is typically vague.

When tax law concerned primarily Western societies, it was possible to ignore or at least to finesse the cultural problem. As countries like China, India, and Brazil become major players it is increasingly difficult to do so. Even countries like France and Italy have a different understanding of the norms of tax administration or the distinction between business and personal expenditures than do the United Kingdom and the United States. When we extend the discussion to Asia or Africa these differences are likely to be magnified many times over. It is possible to consider these differences on a case-by-case basis, or simply take them for granted without ever putting the issue into words. But the need for a more comprehensive approach to the problem seems increasingly obvious.

This book considers the question of tax culture and its implications in a systematic fashion, considering both the work of legal scholars and of experts in other fields – anthropology, sociology, political science, and history – that are relevant to the equation. The book addresses, or attempts to address, a series of closely related questions. What do we mean when we use the term tax culture? How do the tax cultures of various countries differ – is it primarily a matter of attitudes, institutions, or some combination of the two – and how do these differences express themselves in day-to-day tax outcomes? Is tax culture part of the underlying legal or general culture of each individual country or is it independent in nature, and does the answer to this question itself vary between different countries and different time periods? What happens when aspects of one country's tax culture are transferred ("transplanted") to another country, either by force or by voluntary acceptance on the part of the receiving country? What role do international organizations, including more formal ones like the European Union or OECD and less formal ones like the international tax programs at major American universities, play in the development and diffusion of tax culture? Is culture more influential in some areas of tax law than others, and in some countries than others? How does the rise of non-Western countries like China and India affect the equation above? What are the implications of these questions for the so-called convergence or "harmonization" of tax systems and the overall globalization process?

The questions addressed in this book are at once theoretical and practical in nature. On a theoretical level the problem of tax culture is part of the more general question of legal culture – what is more ceremoniously called "law and anthropology" or "law and sociology" in the legal academy – and (specifically) the issue of legal transplants and legal adaptation that lies at the core of comparative law. The work of nontax legal scholars, including Schlesinger, Zweigert and Kötz[1], and others, is thus relevant to the equation, together with that of cultural anthropologists like Margaret Mead, Ruth Benedict, Clifford Geertz, and other less famous but no less significant scholars.[2] Likewise, the work of many tax scholars, from recent authors like Omri Marian and Carlo Garbarino to other more traditional sources, makes an

[1] See Rudolf Schlesinger, Ugo Mattei, Teemu Ruskola, & Antonio Gidi, *Comparative Law: Cases, Texts, Materials* (7th ed.) (New York: Foundation Press, 2009); Konrad Zweigert & Hein Kötz, *An Introduction to Comparative Law* (3rd ed.) (Oxford University Press, 1998).

[2] See, e.g., Margaret Mead, *Coming of Age in Samoa* (New York: W. Morrow & Co., 1928); Ruth Benedict, *Patterns of Culture* (Boston: Houghton Mifflin, 1959); Clifford Geertz, *The Interpretation of Cultures: Selected Essays* (New York: Basic Books, 1973). On the often uneasy relationship between anthropology and law, see Leonard J. Pospisil, *Anthropology of Law:*

important contribution.[3] Yet many of these previous efforts remain incomplete and – perhaps because of the assumption that tax principles are universal in nature – the theoretical framework in the tax field frequently lags behind that in other disciplines. Much of the book will accordingly consist of the expansion or stitching together of ideas from various fields, applying them to areas that may not have been of particular interest to the original authors or of which they were largely unaware. Inevitably we will disagree with some previous scholars altogether. Still, the work of these scholars is invaluable, and this book should be seen as an effort to build upon their thinking rather than to ignore or refute it.

On a practical level, tax culture is simply a more systematic way of stating what we mean when we say that tax systems are different in different places or that tax actors approach their responsibilities in a different manner. Everyone has heard (or made) statements like "tax evasion is more common in Italy than Sweden" or "antitax sentiment is stronger in the United States than in Canada." Somewhat more sophisticated observers may have heard, or made, assertions like "the Chinese tax system tends to favor administrative over judicial resolution of problems" or "Israeli tax administration reflects a mixture of British colonial influence and the country's own Middle Eastern heritage." Other than as clever cocktail-party chatter, what is the significance of these observations? Is it possible or desirable to combine them into a more comprehensive system, in which the components of tax culture could be identified and a series of questions (if not necessarily answers) relevant to all countries developed? Could (couldn't) a more comprehensive framework be useful to those who observe and advise different countries in the design and functioning of their tax systems: those who sense intuitively that what works in one place may not work in another, but who lack a common language and methodology for explaining why? Is there something uniquely impenetrable about individual tax systems, or should (shouldn't) they be subject to description in the same manner as other national characteristics?

## 1.1 TAX AND CULTURE: SOME POSSIBLE OBJECTIONS

Before starting out it may be useful to consider some possible objections to the study of tax and culture. One frequent objection is that tax culture – or the idea of culture in general – is too squishy and too indeterminate in nature: being essentially unquantifiable in character, it can be used to justify almost anything the speaker wants to. (Think of 1930s-era guidebooks that described Nazi uniforms as part of

A *Comparative Theory* (New Haven: HRAF Press, 1974); Sally F. Moore (ed.), *Law and Anthropology: A Reader* (New York: Wiley-Blackwell, 2004).

3 Carlo Garbarino, "An Evolutionary and Structural Approach to Comparative Taxation: Methods and Agenda for Research," *American Journal of Comparative Law*, 57 (2009), 677; Omri Marian, "The Discursive Failure in Comparative Tax Law," *American Journal of Comparative Law*, 58 (2010), 415. A full-length, up-to-date source on comparative tax law is Reuven Avi-Yonah, Nicola Sartori, & Omri Marian, *Global Perspectives on Income Taxation Law* (Oxford University Press, 2011).

German culture, or the argument than racism or misogyny is a "cultural" trait of certain immigrant groups.) This argument is not easily dismissed. Culture may indeed serve to rationalize bad behavior, and has sometimes been used this way in the past. It must always be remembered that to describe a culture, including your own, is not necessarily to accept it.

Yet the alternative of ignoring cultural differences – of pretending that a universal (and typically an American or European model) applies in all times and places – is surely worse than studying them. Just because something is not reducible to numbers does not mean it is insignificant. If it were, we would not bother to teach history, literature, philosophy, or (for that matter) tax policy. The key here is to retain a detached and rational eye in describing what are at bottom irrational or at least nonrational phenomena, and to maintain a healthy humility in distinguishing that which is immutable from that which is subject to change. This is a challenge for scholars, but hardly an impossible one.

A somewhat more sophisticated version of this argument concerns the role of the tax scholar. Even if countries differ, the argument runs, the scholar's role should be to reduce rather than exacerbate these differences, elaborating common themes in a way that will ultimately cause national tax systems to converge around the best common traits. This indeed is the role of many comparative scholars who – while surely aware of the differences between tax systems – focus on identifying the "correct" rules that they hope will eventually be reflected in all regional or national legislation. Indeed, identifying ideal norms and thus improving national legal systems is one of the classic goals of comparative law.[4]

The problem with this objection is twofold. First, it ignores the descriptive as opposed to normative aspect of legal (especially comparative law) scholarship. Before one can change something, one has to know what she is changing and what its place is in the broader legal framework of the country or region at issue. Culture being an inseparable part of tax law and administration, a complete description of taxation can hardly ignore the cultural element. The difference between stated and effective tax rates – that is, the tax rates once we take into account enforcement patterns and individual taxpayer behavior in the country at issue – is a classic example of this problem.

The second problem relates to the identification of the correct or "best" rule. It is an axiom of cultural studies that there is no single, privileged position from which to evaluate the attitudes, beliefs, or institutions of another society.[5] Neutral or universal tax rules frequently turn out, on examination, to reflect a particular, usually Anglo-American or northwest European viewpoint. Understanding the cultural and historical bases of different rules and practices – which of these are indeed universal in nature and which are dependent upon unique, even quirky cultural circumstances –

[4] A classic, if dated, statement of this purpose is Myres S. McDougal, "The Comparative Study of Law For Policy Purposes," *American Journal of Comparative Law*, 1 (1952), 24.

[5] This issue is discussed further in Chapter 2.

is accordingly a prerequisite to serious reform. This is true of all areas of law, but no less so of tax provisions.

A cultural approach involves respect for human differences and (inevitably) a certain level of doubt regarding the standardization of law around a uniform set of values or practices. It will thus be no surprise that I retain a healthy skepticism regarding the convergence of legal and tax systems and – what is essentially the same thing – the "globalization" of tax on an essentially liberal, Western model. Yet celebrating difference is in the end as sterile and simplistic as hailing the end of history or the triumph of universal values. The key is to avoid preconceptions and to distinguish, as systematically as possible, between themes that are common to all societies and those that are not. As in any comparative study, the answers to these questions are likely to be elusive and incomplete. But asking them is half the battle.

## 1.2 LAW AND CULTURE: PREVIOUS SCHOLARLY EFFORTS

Culture has been defined as "the integrated pattern of human knowledge, belief, and behavior that depends upon the capacity for transmitting knowledge to succeeding generations." An alternate definition is "the customary beliefs, social forms, and material traits of a racial, religious, or social group," while still another is "the set of shared attitudes, values, goals, and practices that characterizes an institution or organization," for which is provided the beguiling example of "a corporate culture focused on the bottom line."

Still further definitions involve the acquisition of knowledge or discernment in science, art, and music – what is colloquially called "high culture" or "cultural sophistication."[6] This is what we mean, for example, when we say that one individual is more cultured than another, or that one visits a museum or gallery in order to acquire more culture. These latter definitions are less relevant for our purposes, although they are not wholly without significance.

Cultural studies are most frequently identified with the anthropology field, although they show up in other disciplines as well. While cultural studies are frequently macroscopic in nature – think Margaret Mead in Samoa or Max Weber on the Protestant ethic – there is an equally active interest in the study of social, ethnic, and regional subcultures, including those limited to a specific industry, profession, or economic activity. This is what people mean when they speak of "the culture of the corporate law firm," or make statements such as "the culture of American law schools tends to reward scholarship as opposed to teaching quality." While these statements sometimes reflect an unscientific, pop sensibility, there is an impressive and growing body of academic studies regarding institutional or professional cultures in law and other fields. What these studies lack in breadth and grandeur they compensate for in depth and detail – the "thick description," in the

[6] Webster's Online Dictionary www.merriam-webster.com/dictionary/culture.

memorable phrase of Clifford Geertz, that is easier to achieve in studying a small group or institution than an entire society.[7] If the dictionary definition of culture emphasizes values, attitudes, and beliefs, these microscopic studies focus attention on institutional structures, the subtle or not-so-subtle allocation of rewards, punishments, and responsibilities that makes (say) a Canadian law faculty different from an Italian one, or the process of resolving a tax dispute different in China and the United States. Anyone who has ever dressed for an interview is instinctively aware of these differences.

The problem of culture is of course not unknown to legal scholars, particularly in comparative law. The question is what, exactly, to do about it. The most common historical answer has been not so much to ignore cultural differences as to restrict their sphere of importance, and focus attention on that which is common to different legal systems rather than that which divides them. The operative phrase here is *praesumptio similitudinis*, Latin for "presumption of similarity," which suggests that the many obvious differences between legal systems – democratic versus nondemocratic, civil versus common law, and so forth – mask equally and perhaps more fundamental similarities that will be revealed to the researcher upon further analysis. For example, while the British and American legal systems classify "torts" and "contracts" as common law subjects having essentially judge-made law, and the French and Italian treat both subjects as subdivisions of a legislated "civil code," all four must eventually deal with similar real-world occurrences and – if analyzed according to their substance rather than their form – will reveal significant common themes that allow the (inevitably smaller) differences between them to be isolated and understood. The presumption of similarity lies at the core of the so-called functional method of comparative law, which emphasizes the common problems faced by different legal systems rather than their superficially different ways of approaching them, and which – notwithstanding various challenges – remains the premiere methodology in the field.[8]

Both the presumption of similarity and the functional method marked important advances in comparative legal studies, and the field as we know it would not have existed without them. The only problem with them is that, by and large, they don't work. As Richard Hyland notes in his epic study of the law of gifts, the differences between cultures are by no means uniformly trivial in nature, and the fact that they all face common problems – food, clothing, shelter, or the legal rules pertaining to the gratuitous transfer of property – does not mean that they understand or approach the problems in anything like the same way.[9] The substantive nature of cultural

7 The phrase is taken from the first chapter of Geertz, *Interpretation*, 2, although it has been developed further by several subsequent authors.

8 The functional method is tied to functionalism as a social science (and specifically sociological) tool, which is in turn only one of many intellectual approaches. This issue is discussed further in Chapter 3.

9 Richard Hyland, *Gifts: A Study in Comparative Law* (Oxford University Press, 2009). As the title suggests, the bulk of Hyland's book concerns the treatment of gifts. However, the first chapter of the book contains a useful summary of comparative law doctrine and its limitations.

differences becomes especially significant when we move beyond the North Atlantic countries to embrace Asia, Africa, the Middle East, and other regions that are increasingly important in legal and economic affairs. I might with some difficulty be convinced that the United Kingdom and France share common historical roots and that the differences between them, however significant they appear at first glance, are ultimately less important than the prevailing similarities. It would be harder to convince me that this was true of the UK and Japan, or (for that matter) Israel and Egypt. Yet the latter are increasingly the comparisons that scholars are required to make, particularly in the comparative law field.

A somewhat more sophisticated definition of legal culture is offered by Lawrence Friedman in his book *The Legal System: A Social Science Foundation.*[10] Friedman notes that the term "legal culture" is used in different ways, at times to refer to popular attitudes and behaviors, and at times to describe the values and ideologies of legal professionals (lawyers, judges, etc.) who are most actively involved in the day-to-day administration of justice. The author notes further that, while there are clearly many superficial differences between legal systems, there is a debate as to how significant these differences are and (closely related) whether than to what extent legal systems are converging with the passage of time.[11] Finally, Friedman addresses the question of "modernism" in legal culture, although finding here again that there is no agreement as to what constitutes modernity and how best to achieve it[12].

With so many contested notions, is the concept of legal culture beneficial at all? At least one critic (Roger Cotterrell) has suggested that it is not, to which Friedman responds that a concept may still be useful as a description of reality even though it is difficult to define and even more difficult to quantify.[13] (Think of "quality of life," "love," or for that matter, "God.") This book proceeds, à la Friedman, from the assumption that culture is indeed worth studying, but with a recognition that it can be rather squishy in practice and that one must always be careful about how the word is being used. With this in mind, we will try not to get too far into semantics and to test the term repeatedly against real-world developments.

## 1.3 LAW AND CULTURE: APPLICATION TO THE TAX FIELD

Perhaps because of its relative youth, the tax field is relatively undeveloped in terms of legal theory. The income tax is at most two or three hundred years old; in many countries (including the United States) it has been around for barely a century. Tax law in all countries is primarily statutory in nature, so that the distinction between

[10] New York: The Russell Sage Foundation (1975). Friedman's work is discussed here because of its relevance to the overall structure of the book. A more detailed discussion of law and anthropology is included in Chapter 2.

[11] Lawrence Friedman, *The Legal System*, 193–222.

[12] Ibid.

[13] See R. Cotterrell, "The Concept of Legal Culture," and L. Friedman, A Reply, in David Nelken, *Comparing Legal Cultures* (Abingdon-on-Thames: Routledge Press, 2017).

common and civil law, and perhaps that between positivist and natural law theories, seems less pertinent than in other fields. These factors suggest that tax law would vary relatively little between different cultures, or that such differences as do exist could be analyzed with a common set of legal and economic tools. Yet simple observation tells us that tax systems vary enormously, not only in the taxes imposed but in the level of compliance and the sophistication (not to say enthusiasm) with which the rules are enforced. Observation likewise confirms that taxation is among the most politically contested, emotional areas of law: entire countries, again including the United States, have been born in tax revolts, and some are in danger of dying from them. It is likewise apparent that these differences are not merely economic, but political, historical, and (yes) cultural in nature: the United States and Italy are both advanced industrial or postindustrial countries, but only the most extreme globalist would suggest that their tax systems were substantively identical.

The contradictory features of the tax field have placed comparative tax scholars in an awkward position. By and large they have responded in three ways. The first – consistent with the functionalist tradition – is to emphasize similarities and to leave historical or cultural differences essentially at the margins. This is the approach taken by most textbooks on comparative tax law, which typically describe various countries' rules pertaining to income, deductions, and other matters while making only a relatively limited effort to describe the tax history of the country in question or the relationship of its tax and other laws.[14] Online sources, which have proliferated in recent years, take a similar approach. These works are useful for tax planning but somewhat less so for achieving a genuine understanding of tax systems.

A second, more sophisticated approach takes account of tax culture but tends to define it primarily in attitudinal terms, specifically regarding taxpayer attitudes toward compliance/tax evasion and considering the effect of such attitudes on the design and functioning of national tax systems. The work of Ann Mumford, who has written extensively on tax culture and gender issues, is especially identified with this approach.[15] This work has vastly increased our understanding of the compliance problem, but falls somewhat short of a systematic definition of tax culture.

In recent years there has been an effort to construct a more developed theoretical framework for comparative taxation, spearheaded by a group of Israeli, Italian, and (to a lesser degree) American scholars. The most comprehensive approach is found in the book *Global Perspectives on Income Taxation Law* (2011), coauthored by Reuven Avi-Yonah, Nicola Sartori, and Omri Marian.[16] While most of the book concerns practical issues, the first chapter provides an inventory of existing

[14] See, e.g., Brian J. Arnold & Hugh J. Ault, *Comparative Income Taxation* (3rd ed.) (New York: Aspen Publishers, 2010) Also in this general vein, albeit more detailed, is Victor Thuronyi, *Comparative Tax Law* (Dordrecht, Netherlands: Kluwer Law International, 2003).

[15] See Ann Mumford, *Taxing Cultures: Toward a Theory of Tax Collection Law* (London: Ashgate Publishers, 2002).

[16] Avi-Yonah, Sartori, & Marian, *Global Perspectives*.

theoretical approaches including functional, cultural, and critical methods, and a fourth method emphasizing economic analysis. Professor Marian has written a separate article critiquing functional and other approaches and attempts to connect them to broader developments in comparative law generally.[17] With characteristic bluntness, he suggests that previous scholars have "failed to produce even the faintest form of paradigmatic discourse," arguably an overstatement of the problem but not very much so.

Also significant is the work of Carlo Garbarino, who has proposed a "functional evolutionary" approach emphasizing themes of institutional analysis, tax transplants, and an effort to identify a "common core" of tax principles across national boundaries.[18] Garbarino differs from Marian in having greater European emphasis and, perhaps, in being somewhat less skeptical about the functionalist method. But their work is to a large degree complementary, with each noting the limitation of current approaches and attempting to update tax law for developments in other areas.

The work of Garbarino, Marion, Avi-Yonah, and others suggests that a more systematic approach to comparative tax law, which moves beyond simple description to take account of developments in other fields, may at last be in the offing. But – as these authors would no doubt concede – much work remains to be done. In particular, three important questions remain unanswered.

First, at the risk of repetition, there remains a need for a more comprehensive and inclusive definition of tax culture. While the word culture is frequently used by tax scholars, in practice it refers primarily to taxpayer attitudes and surveys reflecting those attitudes. The institutional side of culture – how are tax laws made and enforced, what is the role and training of various professionals (lawyers, accountants, economists) in the lawmaking process, how did the country's tax institutions develop, and what is the role of historical factors in understanding tax outcomes – tends to be much less developed, even in the Western countries themselves. Since institutional factors frequently dominate and often help to shape attitudinal differences, this is a significant omission.[19]

Second, and closely related, there is a need for a more robust and realistic approach to the convergence problem. It is a truism that the world is becoming smaller and that tax and other legal systems are becoming more like one another. Conventional wisdom likewise suggests that where convergence does not take place, it is because of deep-seated differences in values and attitudes that are not subject to the globalization process. Yet each of these assumptions is to a certain degree false: tax systems remain very different from one another, and these differences frequently result from institutional or historical factors rather than profound or deep-seated national values. Indeed, these latter factors may sometimes be more intractable than

17 Marian, "The Discursive Failure."

18 Garbarino, "An Evolutionary and Structural Approach."

19 See Chapter 3.

popular attitudes, which are often quite malleable. What is the role of such factors in restraining or accelerating the legal convergence process and how should scholars respond to them?

Finally, a comprehensive approach must recognize the ongoing changes in the allocation of global influence. Even the more recent works on comparative taxation tend to have a European, or European-American, emphasis. The rise of China, India, and other non-European powers suggests that this approach is no longer viable. How does the Asian perspective on taxation differ from that of the traditional powers, and what effect will this have on the global tax system? Do these differences express themselves primarily through attitudes, institutions, or some combination of the two, and which if either of these differences are subject to the convergence process? How has the rise of transnational tax institutions – both formal ones like the OECD and informal ones like academic exchange programs – affected the behavior of non-Western tax systems, and how in turn have these institutions been affected by non-Western countries?

## 1.4 COROLLARY ISSUES I: NATURAL LAW, POSITIVISM, AND THE TAX FIELD

The issue of legal culture is distinct from, but closely related to, several other issues in legal philosophy. One of the most important concerns the division between positivism and natural law, at one time the defining issue in legal philosophy. While not quite as prominent today, it still possesses significant influence.

Natural law, which has origins and religion and philosophy, suggests that there are certain immutable principles that will exist under any just legal system. For example, the prohibitions against murder and incest are often cited as universal rules that transcend the differences between legal systems. By contrast, positivism suggests that law consists of the rules promulgated by the sovereign – that is, the "positive law" – whatever an outsider might think of those rules. Put in simplest terms, natural law assumes a convergence between law and morality, while positive law does not. Most observers probably fall somewhere between these two extremes: even a positivist might accept that certain laws (e.g., those protecting slavery) had dubious legal status, while most natural law advocates would probably profess to at least some humility in defining universal principles. As a general rule, positivism is dominant in the legal academy, but with natural law making something of a comeback in recent years.[20]

Perhaps because of its statutory origins, tax law tends heavily toward the positivist side of the equation. No one has seriously claimed that the income tax was given on

[20] For a useful introduction to positivist legal theory, see Hans Kelsen, *Pure Theory of Law* (Berkeley: University of California Press, 1967) (original German edition published in 1934). For a recent example of a natural law approach, see Robert George, *In Defense of Natural Law* (Oxford: Clarendon Press, 1999).

Mount Sinai, or that the distinction between capital gain and ordinary income is part of the natural order. Yet some religious observers have claimed, for example, that a 10-percent tax – the biblical tithe – is divinely ordained, while others have claimed that higher, redistributive taxes are necessary to achieve a biblical standard of social justice. Similar claims have been made for the poor tax (*zakat*) in Islamic countries. These claims give tax law something of a natural law flavor, although arguably not to the extent of criminal law, family law, or other areas that regularly make appeals to religious principles.

Natural law-style claims become more common if one moves from religion, as traditionally defined, to secular philosophy. Thus, fairness, efficiency, and simplicity have been dubbed the "holy trinity" of tax policy, and certain features of the income tax, like the Haig-Simons definition of income and the distinction between personal and business expenditures, have come to be seen as natural or inevitable features of a just tax system. Just how universal these principles really are, and how dependent on cultural factors that vary between different societies, is an important theme of this book.

## 1.5 COROLLARY ISSUES II: CIVIL AND COMMON LAW

Closely related to the issue of natural law and positivism is the question of families of law and their usefulness in classifying legal systems. The most common classification is, of course, the distinction between civil and common law, the latter typical of the United Kingdom, United States, and other English-speaking jurisdictions, and the former of Continental Europe and its former colonies. Although there are many differences between civil and common law, most of them relate to the source of law question, the principal sources of law being statutory in civil law countries and (until recently) judicial decisions in common law jurisdictions. Many other differences between these systems, including interpretive styles, the role of precedent, and the relative prestige of judges and legal scholars derive from this original difference.

Perhaps the most comprehensive effort at defining families of law is contained in Konrad Zweigert and Hein Kötz's justifiably classic work *An Introduction to Comparative Law*. Not content with the civil versus common law distinction, Zweigert and Kötz suggest the existence of no fewer than seven distinct families of law, including separate French and German spheres of influence together with British Law, American Law, Islamic and Hindu Law, Law of the Far East, and so forth. Interestingly for our own later purposes, the authors treat Scandinavian Law as a separate family rather than including it in Germanic Law or one of the other categories. Also of later interest, Zweigert and Kötz resist the frequent tendency to dismiss non-Western cultures as either inferior or outside of law altogether – a strong temptation for lawyers even if it holds little sway for anthropologists and other social scientists – although they recognize the significant differences between Western and non-Western systems. (Zweigert and Kötz are also important in developing the presumption of similarity and the functional method, as described above.)[21]

The distinction between civil and common law has perhaps less influence on tax than other legal disciplines. Because tax law (especially income tax law) is largely a twentieth-century phenomenon – and because it is almost universally statutory in origin, even in common law jurisdictions – there is a sense that it is less affected by the broader legal system than (say) tort or contract law. Yet this similarity can easily be overstated. For example, although US tax law is nominally statutory, in practice numerous issues from the definition of income (sec. 61 of the Internal Revenue Code) to the rules for tax-exempt mergers (sec. 368) are controlled by judicial decisions. Indeed, many current tax statutes – section 119 is one obvious example – were effectively responses to previous judicial decisions. These phenomena would be much less likely in a civil law country. The use of precedent in tax cases and the constitutional review of tax-related cases also vary significantly between civil and common law systems.

The teaching of tax, like other subjects, is likewise different in civil and common law countries, emphasizing a deductive, law-to-facts approach in the former and an inductive, facts-to-law kind of reasoning in the latter. The first case in my own (common law) casebook concerns a hotel manager whom the Internal Revenue Service tried unsuccessfully to tax on the value of his food and lodging at a Hawaiian, pre-Pearl Harbor resort.[22] Nobody really cares about the manager, who has presumably been dead for a long time anyway: the idea is for students to deduce the fringe benefit taxation rules from a series of improbable, bizarre fact patterns. (Some succeed at this and some inevitably don't.) Other cases involve similarly bizarre circumstances, some of which I myself have difficulty remembering from year to year.

In contrast, Italian law students begin by asking basic, underlying questions (What is a tax? Who qualifies as a taxpayer? What is mean by taxpaying capacity?), proceeding methodically through the tax or other equivalent code and only rarely considering actual fact circumstances. Judicial decisions (*giurisprudenza*) are less important to these students than the statements (*dottrina*) of learned, or supposedly learned, scholars. The ways that these students think about tax problems are likely to be quite different, even if many of the rules are the same.

Even if they do not constitute separate legal families, differences in legal and political culture can have profound tax significance. In China, I noticed that tax policy issues – fairness, efficiency, progressive or flat taxation – were typically discussed in terms of their effect on the overall society rather than their impact on

21 Zweigert & Kötz, *An Introduction*.

22 *Benaglia* v. *Commissioner*, 36 B.T.A. 838 (1937).

individual taxpayers. In Israel, any tax discussion seemed to turn very quickly toward ethnic differences (Jews and Arabs, religious and secular Jews) and the impact of tax policy on these different groups. In Nordic countries, concerns of simplicity and efficient administration were frequently paramount, although these were not always achieved in practice. These and similar phenomena are discussed further in Chapter 5.

## 1.6 PUTTING MEAT ON THE BONES: WHERE WE GO FROM THERE

The remainder of this book addresses the questions above in greater detail. Chapters 2 and 3 attempt to construct a comprehensive definition of tax culture, including both attitudinal issues (primarily Chapter 3) and institutional factors (Chapter 3). Attitudinal issues include cultural norms regarding tax evasion and tax compliance; the role of the state in the economy; the balance between individual and collective goals; and related matters. Institutional factors include the tax legislative and administrative processes; the education of tax professionals; and the influence of supranational organizations on domestic tax policy. The role of historical quirks or accidents, like the colonial legacy in Israel or India and the history of tax revolts in the United States, is also considered here. At the conclusion of Chapter 3 the tax systems of the Nordic countries, which have some similarities to those of the English-speaking countries but also many profound differences, are described in further detail.

Chapter 4 considers the problem of convergence and divergence of tax systems and the role of culture in this process. Recent decades have seen an effort to develop transnational tax norms by direct action (as in the case of the European Union and other international bodies) or informal means (educational programs, "model" tax codes, and the activities of the OECD and similar groups). The work of comparative tax scholars has also tended to support a convergence model. Yet these efforts have frequently met with frustration, because countries differ in their underlying political beliefs and because their differing institutions ensure that rules which start out similarly will ultimately take different paths. The work of several previous scholars, notably Allison Christians on international tax bodies, Ruth Mason on the European Union, and Assaf Likhovski with respect to tax avoidance rules form a starting point for this chapter.[23]

Chapter 5 considers geographic patterns in tax law and whether it is possible to delineate families of tax law as in other areas. In particular, this chapter considers the "Asian Century" and its impact on the comparative tax field. The rise of China and India, likely to be the two largest economies in the world within the next generation, is considered in particular detail. China and India differ from the West (and each

[23] See, e.g., Allison Christians, "Networks, Norms and National Tax Policy," *Washington University Global Studies Law Review*, 9 (2010), 1; Assaf Likhovski, "The Duke and the Lady: Helvering v. Gregory and the History of Tax Avoidance Adjudication," *Cardozo Law Review*, 25 (2004), 953.

other) in both attitudes and institutions, ranging from the Chinese emphasis on collective goals (e.g., "harmony") over individual rights and preference for administrative over judicial decision-making to the combination of British institutions and Hindu philosophy that coexist uneasily in an Indian context. The question of tax transplants is especially salient here: while non-Western nations have traditionally adjusted to Western tax norms, the size and influence of these two countries suggests that the adjustment may be in the opposite direction. The role of organized religion in tax policy – at times marginal but never irrelevant – is also considered.

Chapter 6 moves from theory to practice, considering three case studies – the problem of income tax progressivity, the issue of tax avoidance, and the rise of environmental taxes – and how they reflect the themes above. While each of these problems is universal in nature, in practice their resolution depends heavily on cultural factors. Thus, progressive taxation in the United States – while seeming to contradict the country's individualist spirit – is protected by a variety of institutional barriers, while in several more collectivist countries it is undermined by weaker traditions of tax compliance and tax administration. Similarly, strategies to combat tax avoidance vary considerably depending upon taxpayer attitudes, the balance of individual rights and government authority, and the allocation of lawmaking power between administrative, judicial, and legislative branches. Environmental taxes are strong in the Nordic countries and some other areas, but much weaker in the world as a whole. Here as in previous chapters, the role of historical quirks and anomalies remains significant, and the convergence of tax systems is frequently more formal than substantive in nature. This chapter also considers the clash between tax and nontax law in areas, such as environmental or family tax, where tax and nontax rules overlap most forcefully.

Chapter 7 evaluates the theoretical questions originally posed in Chapter 1 in light of the intervening discussion. While tax law has several unique features, the need for a comprehensive definition of legal culture which includes both institutional and attitudinal factors is applicable in all legal fields. A judicious skepticism regarding the "globalization" of law and the "convergence" of legal cultures is likewise justified beyond the tax area. Tax law, which has historically lagged behind other subjects in theoretical sophistication, may thus provide a guidepost for future developments in both the theory and practice of comparative law.

# 2

# Tax Anthropology: Attitudes, Behaviors, and the Role of Historical Contingencies

As observed in Chapter 1, the definition of culture is complicated, calling to mind Justice Potter Stewart's admonition that he could never quite define pornography but "I know it when I see it." For convenience, we may divide culture into its attitudinal aspects – the knowledge, belief, and behavior part of the definition in Chapter 1 – and its institutional component, which concerns the values and practices that characterize a particular institution or organization. Of course, these two aspects overlap in practice since institutional structures are founded on knowledge while beliefs are determined to a large degree by the institutional structures in which they arise; yet the distinction remains useful.

In discussing culture, there is a widespread tendency to emphasize attitudinal rather than institutional aspects. For example, tourists will frequently make statements like "Germans are efficient" or "Italians love opera" without much considering the historical or institutional factors that contribute to these attitudes, or even if they are objectively true. In the tax field, it is common to hear that "Americans hate the income tax" or "Scandinavians are more progressive than Anglo-Saxons," once again without considering institutional contexts or (frequently) providing much evidence in support of the statement. This tendency is unfortunate, both because it inverts reality – institutions are frequently more important than and often determinative of popular attitudes – and because it leads to a certain laziness in the evaluation of national and local characteristics. (Americans actually tolerate a surprisingly progressive income tax system, while Scandinavian business taxes are frequently lower than in the United States.) There is a related but distinct tendency to confuse popular attitudes with those of the relatively small elite that makes and enforces tax policy, a confusion not limited to taxes.

Notwithstanding these limitations – and allowing for a healthy skepticism regarding the validity of the attitudes/institutions dichotomy – for convenience's sake we will begin our survey with the question of taxpayer attitudes, leaving the question of tax institutions for Chapter 3. In particular, we will consider three aspects of this problem: attitudes toward progressive or redistributive taxation; the question of tax compliance; and the related but distinct issue of antitax political movements. Before embarking upon this venture, it is worth a brief detour regarding the work of anthropologists and their approach to the broader problem of culture.

## 2.1 A (MUCH TOO BRIEF) DIGRESSION: THE WORLD OF CULTURAL ANTHROPOLOGY

If anthropology is "the science of human beings," cultural anthropology is the subdivision that deals primarily with culture. For lawyers, culture is a mushy, undefined term: but there is an entire field of study organized around it, and many who have devoted their lives to its pursuit. There is likewise a significant literature on law and anthropology, although relatively little of it concerns the tax field.

Anthropology conjures up images of primitive tribes on far-away islands, and indeed much important anthropological research has taken place in such settings, a circumstance that results less from anthropologists' taste for the exotic (although that is not wholly insignificant) than from the need to observe different cultures in order to understand one's own. One thinks of Margaret Mead's work in Samoa; Ruth Benedict's research on natives of New Guinea or the Pacific Northwest; Clifford Geertz's description of cockfighting in Bali; and other scholars who have spent years studying the work, play, marriage and courtship rituals, and other behavior patterns of tribes that might have remained largely unknown except for their efforts.[1] The contributions of these scholars are justifiably world-famous.

The goal of cultural anthropology is not, or is not only, to increase our understanding of the societies in question, but to demonstrate that attitudes and institutions which appear natural or inevitable to Westerners are in fact only one of a series of possible alternatives that have been adopted by different societies at different times and in different conditions. (This is, in essence, merely a restatement of the proposition that one must understand another society in order to appreciate one's own.) Mead's work on adolescence in Samoa is perhaps the most famous example of this phenomenon: although criticized on various grounds, it helped to establish the fact that Western norms of adolescence, family, and gender were not universal in nature, and had a significant if at times ambiguous impact on American and European perceptions in this area. Benedict's and Geertz's work, if slightly less famous, has a similar effect. I can no longer think of the competition between law schools without referencing Benedict's work on the potlaches of the Northwest Indians, nor watch a football game without thinking of Geertz's description of the rules, written and unwritten, for observing a Balian cockfight.

[1] See, e.g., Margaret Mead, *Coming of Age in Samoa* (New York: W. Morrow & Co., 1928); Ruth Benedict, *Patterns of Culture* (Boston: Houghton Mifflin, 1934); Clifford Geertz, *The Interpretation of Cultures: Selected Essays* (New York: Basic Books, 1973).

Cultural anthropology is a vast and ever-changing field, and describing or even summarizing its principal accomplishments is a task well beyond the scope of this book. But a few essential points bear mentioning.

First, it is a basic tenet of cultural anthropology that, while all cultures perceive and promote significance in life – what Ruth Benedict calls "meaning" – their understanding of what is significant varies enormously, and will frequently be unintelligible to those outside their cultural system.[2] From this perspective, the assertion that all societies promote, or ought to promote, the same values is merely a reflection of one's own cultural perspective and may be of little value in understanding what actually happens in those societies. This seems like an obvious point, but it can easily be overlooked: consider, for example, the common assumption that all societies seek (or ought to seek) the achievement of higher per capita incomes, or that economic goals are universal and objective in character while religious or political values are essentially subjective and local. Indeed, the entire concept of universal values would seem odd to an anthropologist, who would be likely to see them as the values of one group which had been adopted by, or forced upon, another. Even the Ten Commandments, as Sanford Levinson memorably pointed out, can mean different things in different cultural settings.[3]

A second and related tenet is that, however strongly we may feel otherwise, there is no neutral perspective from which to evaluate different cultures or assert that one's own culture is "better" or "more advanced" than someone else's. This is true because the values that we would apply in making this claim are necessarily cultural in nature: there is no "acultural" vantage point from which to assert or defend such a claim. That doesn't mean that values aren't important, or that numerous values have not, as a historical matter, come to be shared by different societies. Most of us would probably agree that racism is a bad thing and that murder or cannibalism are, as a general rule, bad ideas. Many of us would, I assume, refuse to live in a society that engaged in or rationalized these practices. But these remain culturally based values.

Finally, cultural anthropology is strongly identified with the value of detailed observation – what Clifford Geertz famously termed "thick description" – as a methodological approach. The oft-heard criticism in law school faculty lounges, that someone's work is "merely descriptive" and not sufficiently normative in nature, would be all but unintelligible in anthropological circles. Geertz's own work, in which he goes to extraordinary lengths describing the organization, structure, and betting patterns in Balinese cockfighting matches, is a classic case in point: while not devoid of analysis, the piece is overwhelmingly descriptive in nature and simply assumes that the knowledge acquired will be of value at some future time.[4]

2 Benedict, *Patterns*, 1.

3 Sanford V. Levinson, "On Interpretation: The Adultery Clause of the Ten Commandments," *Southern California Law Review*, 56 (1985), 719.

4 "Deep Play: Notes on the Balinese Cockfight" in Geertz, *The Interpretation*, 1, p. 412.

## 2.2 LAW AND ANTHROPOLOGY: STATING THE PROBLEM

From an anthropologist's perspective, what we call "law" is merely an especially systematic and formalized method of social control, which was historically tied to religious or other supernatural sanctions but in more advanced societies has become separate from them. Not surprisingly, the bulk of work on law and anthropology emphasizes substantive areas – family law, criminal law, and the various forms of dispute resolution – that are most closely tied to traditional anthropological research and in which differences between societies are most easily observed. Also unsurprisingly, much of this work concerns non-Western or what used to be called "primitive" societies, although this has changed in recent years.[5]

The biases above have, of course, not stopped scholars in other fields from using terms like "culture" or "anthropology" in their own research. Thus Robert Clark, in an otherwise conventional account of corporate tax law, begins with a lengthy account of the culture of corporate tax lawyers and how it has impacted the development of the field.[6] The present author, in a primarily economic discussion of taxation and risk, has inserted a rather verbose discussion of cultural biases affecting the evaluation of risk and its role in tax policy.[7] These efforts are admirable, but they typically lack methodological sophistication and are frequently unclear as to the definition of culture they are employing or whose behavior and attitudes (the broader society, the political elite, or specific professional organizations) they are talking about. Most discussions of "tax and culture" suffer from similar limitations.

If legal scholars only occasionally use the word "culture," this does not mean that they are not subject to numerous cultural biases. The most common of these is that critiqued above: the assumption that one's own goals and values are shared by people living in other societies and in different time periods. Indeed, the so-called presumption of similarity – the theoretical basis of the entire field of comparative law – is essentially a negation of cultural differences, a point made eloquently by Richard Hyland in his treatise. The assumption that all legal systems should protect individual rights, or all tax systems should promote economic efficiency, are similarly cultural in nature, although they have become so broadly shared that we tend not to notice. Cultural biases are also apparent on a methodological level. Comparative law (and especially comparative tax law) has a tendency toward broad-brushed

5 For a sample of work in this area, see Leonard Pospisil, *Anthropology of Law: A Comparative Theory* (New York: Harper & Row, 1971); Norbert Rouland, *Legal Anthropology* (Stanford University Press, 1994); Lawrence Rosen, *Law as Culture: An Invitation* (Princeton University Press, 2006); and David Nelken (ed.), *Comparing Legal Cultures* (England and Vermont: Dartmouth Publishing Company, 1997). In recent years there has been an increasing effort to apply anthropological methods to the study of international business and finance; see, e.g., Annelise Riles, *Collateral Knowledge: Legal Reasoning in the Global Financial Markets* (University of Chicago Press, 2011).

6 Robert C. Clark, "The Morphogenesis of Subchapter C: An Essay in Statutory Evolution and Reform," *Yale Law Journal*, 87 (1977), 90.

7 Michael A. Livingston, "Risky Business: Economics, Culture, and the Taxation of High-Risk Industries," *Tax Law Review*, 48 (1993), 163.

description that is far removed from the methods of Geertz and others in their field work.

In fairness, some degree of cultural bias is inevitable: one can never escape one's own culture entirely, and it is not even completely clear that one should try to. Comparative law scholars have begun paying more attention to non-Western societies and, in a number of cases, attempted "thick" rather than superficial descriptions of other legal systems. Yet the degree of cultural insensitivity, not to say simple intellectual laziness, is often quite remarkable. The advice given by Western lawyers and economists to postcommunist societies, which ignored cultural differences with often tragic results, is an example of this phenomenon. Austerity programs advised or forced upon countries of the developing world by the IMF and other international organizations have been accused of a similar cultural insensitivity, although the point is debated.[8]

In discussing culture, it is important to distinguish between the local, national, and supranational levels. The concept of subcultures is of primary importance here. Thus, as Robert Clark suggests, there may be a culture of tax lawyers whose behavior and attitudes differ from those of the general society. (Try explaining a "B-reorg" to a nonlawyer if you don't believe this.) Tax culture may also be supranational or even global in character: as experts in different countries begin to share common educational and professional experiences, they may come to resemble one another more than ordinary people in their respective countries. At this point, it may be possible to speak of an international as well as national tax cultures, with profound implications for the character and development of tax law. One must be careful not to exaggerate: there are important checks against the universalization of tax policy, and the author remains highly skeptical regarding the "globalization" phenomenon in tax and other areas of public policy. Yet the concept of sub-national and supra-national cultures remains important.

## 2.3 LAW AND ANTHROPOLOGY: SOME PRACTICAL APPLICATIONS

When discussing the practical impact of cultural anthropology, one must begin with the broader relationship of law and social science. This relationship is complicated by the traditional sense of law as an independent field – a science in its own right, so to speak – that does not need or require interference from practitioners of other academic fields. More recently, economics has emerged as a powerful tool in legal analysis, not so much pushing aside as simply ignoring the other social sciences, which can be more difficult to translate into the kinds of seemingly infallible rules of theorems that lawyers historically crave.

[8] Criticisms of the IMF's role in the developing world are by now quite numerous. Two of the better-known examples are Joseph E. Stiglitz, *Globalization and Its Discontents* (New York: W.W. Norton & Co., 2003); and Amy Chua, *World on Fire: How Exporting Free Market Democracy Breeds Ethnic Hatred and Global Instability* (New York and London: Doubleday, 2003).

The influence of economics is most visible in the law and economics movement, which has affected nearly every law faculty in the last generation and come to dominate some of them. Associated most prominently with work of Richard Posner and others at the University of Chicago, this movement has taken a predominantly conservative turn, being used frequently to argue that government regulation is ineffective or even counterproductive in outcome. But economics has also played a significant role in the critical legal studies (CLS) movement, which emphasizes law's role in maintaining and rationalizing the power of dominant economic and political formations in a given society. At least one scholar has suggested that the CLS and law and economics movements are really two sides of the same coin, each emerging from the Legal Realist movement of the 1930s and each suggesting that the "microanalysis" of lawmaking institutions, rather than considerations of legal doctrine, constitutes the proper focus for legal scholars. The Legal Realist movement, in turn, reflected in part the influence of European lawyers and social scientists in the prewar and immediate postwar periods, with their concept of legal science (*rechtswissenschaft*) as a subject to be studied in a systematic, quasi-scientific manner. Whether one likes or laments these movements, much of the intellectual energy in the legal academy has originated with one or another of them.[9]

Anthropology, sociology, psychology, and various humanities disciplines (most notably history and philosophy) have played a significant but until recently more limited role in legal scholarship.[10] Being a largely descriptive field that tends to focus on non-Western societies, anthropology has been perhaps more marginal than the others. Yet law and anthropology is not without its achievements, particularly where comparative law is concerned. While much of this work is of Continental European or émigré origin, in recent years it has enjoyed increasing influence in both the British and North American legal academies.

Modern law and anthropology is sometimes traced to the appearance of Bruno Malinowki's book *Crime and Custom in Savage Society*[11] in 1926. Malinowski studied crime and punishment among the people of the Trobriand Islands of Papua New Guinea, emphasizing the need to compare the functions of law in different cultures rather than searching for discrete legal institutions. Malinowski's other research investigated the role of exchange in primitive society and related subjects. Work in the Malinowski tradition – sometimes called the Anglo-American approach to legal anthropology – has made enormous contributions but is sometimes criticized for its characteristic distinction between primitive and advanced

9 On CLS and Law and Economics' origins in Legal Realism, see Edward L. Rubin, "The New Legal Process, The Synthesis of Discourse, and the Microanalysis of Institutions," *Harvard Law Review*, 109 (1996), 1393.

10 The influence of sociology is discussed in Chapter 3.

11 London: Routledge Press, 1926 (original ed.)

societies, and (in some cases) the suggestion that genuine law exists only in the latter.[12]

A different approach, reflecting a more Continental influence, is Leopold Pospisil's 1971 book *Anthropology of Law: A Comparative Theory*. Pospisil emphasizes three fundamental aspects of law – authority, obligation, and sanction – and their manifestation in three different cultures: the Kapauku Papuans of New Guinea, the Nunamiut Eskimos, and the Alpine Tiroleans of present-day Austria. In particular the book compares the treatment of land tenure and inheritance problems, which are found to vary dramatically between the cultures studied. Following these practical comparisons is a lengthy theoretical chapter on the evolution or change of laws, including the insights of Montesquieu, Marx, Durkheim, and numerous other philosophers, which are then applied to the three peoples studied earlier. Most radical of all is the author's forceful rejection of the argument that law exists only in Western or other "advanced" societies, a rejection which he phrases in characteristically blunt terms: "[T]here is no basic qualitative difference between tribal (primitive) and civilized law."[13]

A still more comprehensive approach is taken by Norbert Rouland in a 1988 book bearing the simple English title *Legal Anthropology*. Rouland reviews previous approaches to legal anthropology (including Pospisil's) and tests them against the experience of several traditional societies, primarily on the African continent. With a stunning degree of detail, Rouland considers subjects ranging from marriage and inheritance to dispute resolution, land tenure, and rules for the formation of contracts in each of the cultures studied. Like Pospisil, Rouland rejects the idea of Western exclusivity or superiority in the legal field; indeed, a major purpose of the book is to reject such ideas, which Rouland associates with colonialism and the forced imposition of Western law in traditional societies.

## 2.4 SMALL BUT NOT FORGOTTEN: CULTURAL ANTHROPOLOGY AND TAXATION

Perhaps because there are few "primitive" societies left to study, anthropologists have more recently turned their attention to Western cultures and subcultures, and to fields like taxation and corporate law that previously escaped their attention. Probably the most prominent exemplar of this trend is Annelise Riles, a lawyer and anthropologist who has studied an astonishing range of subjects from an anthropological perspective. Thus, in her 2011 book *Collateral Knowledge: Legal Reasoning*

12 The difference between advanced and primitive, or Western and non-Western, law is (as one might expect) fraught with controversy. For a sophisticated but somewhat dated argument for the superiority of Western law, see Harold Berman, *Law and Revolution: The Formation of the Western Legal Tradition* (Cambridge: Harvard University Press, 1983).

13 Leopold Pospisil, *Anthropology of Law: A Comparative Theory* (New York: Harper & Row, 1971).

*in the Global Financial Markets*,[14] Riles applies a cultural analysis to international business law, in particular the rules applicable to financial derivatives trading ("swaps") in the United States and Japan. A recurring theme of the book is the difference between American and Japanese legal culture and the way that even the same written rules – many Japanese laws were written during or shortly after the postwar US occupation of Japan – have a different effect because of the interposition of different cultural norms and their effect on day-to-day behavior.[15]

Riles' other work addresses such varied topics as cultural feminism and knowledge practices among international bureaucrats, as well as issues explored in an edited collection, *Documents: Artifacts of Modern Knowledge*,[16] which considers legal and other documents as ethnographic objects and considers what these might tell us about the current state of anthropological and legal theory. Her most recent work considers the politics of international banking and the uneasy relationship between experts and nonexperts in the field.[17]

Another Cornell product, Emily Levitt, applies similar methods closer to home. Levitt's research investigates the Cayuga Indian Nation of New York (CIN) and its strategy of buying up property within the nation's traditional geographic boundaries, leading to predictable disputes with state and local tax authorities. Levitt is especially concerned with the response of local residents to the CIN's efforts and its implications for citizenship, sovereignty, and other symbolic concepts. Although such work differs from the technical emphasis of most legal scholars, it is no less significant for the understanding of underlying tax concepts.[18]

A more esoteric but no less significant line of research relates to the voluntary payment of taxes and how to situate such behavior within traditional human norms. Much of this work traces its way back to the French sociologist Marcel Mauss' 1925 work *The Gift*,[19] which – notwithstanding its title – is primarily a study of voluntary exchanges and their role in establishing and maintaining human relationships. Although more frequently applied in defense of welfare programs, *The Gift* has also inspired a revival of interest in tax compliance, which combines aspects of gift-giving with the concept of a voluntary exchange between individual taxpayers (who pay the taxes) and the government (which provides services and other benefits to them in return). A number of books, papers, and conferences have investigated this issue in recent years.

14 Chicago and London: University of Chicago Press, 2011.

15 Ibid.

16 Ann Arbor: University of Michigan Press, 2006.

17 See Riles, *Collateral Knowledge*, 14.

18 Emily K. Levitt, *Cultures of Sovereignty and Fiscal Order*, doctoral dissertation under direction of Paul Nadasdy, Cornell University, www.anthropology.cornell.edu.

19 *The Gift* was originally published in a French sociology journal in 1925 and later as a book, in French and English, in the 1950s. A more recent edition is Marcel Mauss, *The Gift: The Form and Reason for Exchange in Archaic Societies* (New York: W.W. Norton & Co., 1980).

Of particular interest is a book by the Swedish anthropologist Lotta Björklund Larsen titled *A Fair Share of Tax: A Fiscal Anthropology of Contemporary Sweden.*[20] The book begins with the question of why people pay taxes, but gradually moves beyond to investigate the entire pattern of exchanges and reciprocity created by the tax system of a modern postindustrial nation. Interestingly, Björklund Larsen considers the perspective of both taxpayers and the Swedish tax agency (*Skatteverket*), and conducts extensive conversations both with Swedes who pay their share of taxes and with some who don't, engaging in smaller and larger types of black market (*svartarbet*) transactions that have the intention and effect of avoiding tax. The implication of the latter is clear if disturbing: if people pay taxes because they expect reciprocal benefits, those who believe that the government is not acting in their interests may refuse to pay them, even in an advanced country like Sweden, which is generally believed to have a high level of tax compliance.

## 2.5 TAX CULTURE AND BEHAVIOR: THE PROBLEM OF COMPLIANCE

The term "tax culture" is sometimes used by lawyers and economists as well as anthropologists, but they tend to use it in a different way. For the former groups, the term refers primarily to studies of taxpayer compliance, and it has a more practical emphasis than anthropologists, typically involving quantitative studies of taxpayer behavior in different countries. This focus on such studies is to a degree understandable. Most income tax systems are voluntary in nature, that is, they depend upon the voluntary filing of tax returns by individuals and corporations, although typically imposing penalties on those who fail to do so. It is readily apparent that certain taxpayers, or taxpayers in certain countries, are more likely to comply with this obligation than others. Does this behavior rise to the level of a cultural trait, and (if so) what can countries do to encourage it?

In her book *Taxing Culture* (2002), Ann Mumford examines the culture of tax collection in the United States and the United Kingdom, with an emphasis on the self-assessment of income tax. In a comprehensive and wide-ranging work, Mumford considers both technical tax issues and broader sociological concepts, including the construction of citizenship, the impact of feminist theory, and the relationship between tax simplicity (or complexity) and the success or failure of tax collection efforts. The different tax histories of the two countries – American-style self-assessment of income tax is a relatively recent concept in the UK – are an important theme of the book.

The fall of communism and the introduction of Western-style income tax systems in formerly communist nations have engendered still further studies of taxpayer attitudes. A common theme is the difficulty of establishing a culture of

[20] Basingstoke: Palgrave MacMillan, 1998. The Swedish tax system is discussed further in Chapter 5. The book is also available on open access https://link.springer.com/content/pdf/10.1007%2F978-3-319-69772-7.pdf

taxpayer compliance in countries, such as those of Eastern Europe, that lack a tradition of civic obligation in tax and other matters and in which a high degree of skepticism toward governmental institutions persists. At the opposite extreme, Nordic (Scandinavian) countries have asserted that their taxpayers have a positive attitude toward tax compliance because of the benefits they receive in return for taxes and the service orientation of their countries' tax bureaucracies.[21] These claims are often difficult to prove, but they are not wholly without foundation.

One problem here is that it can be difficult to separate compliance from its underlying social context. For example, it may be logical for Nordic taxpayers to comply with tax rules if the tax system is fair and efficient, and equally logical for Italian taxpayers to avoid compliance if the system is not. Or, it may simply be the case that (say) Swedish tax enforcement is more effective than the Italian variety, so that people comply because tax evasion is more difficult to accomplish successfully rather than because the tax system is fair or equitable. Put differently, it can be difficult to separate attitudes from institutions, and the latter sometimes dictate the former rather than the other way around. We shall have occasion to revisit this problem as the book progresses.

Moving beyond compliance to the whole range of tax behavior and outcomes is the work of the Hamburg-based scholar Birger Nerré. In a series of books and articles Nerré develops a model of tax culture that takes account of tax policy-makers – academics, tax officials, and so forth – as well as individual taxpayers, and which recognizes the ethnic and national differences that underlie even the most simple, basic tax processes.

According to Nerré, tax culture functions at the intersection of economics, sociology, and history and involves the full range of approaches – what Nerré calls mentalities, morale, and discipline – that people apply in approaching tax issues. The failure to take such differences into account can lead to "tax policy shocks," as when the United States attempted to impose aspects of its tax system on postwar Japan, or "tax policy lags," as when Russia tried (unsuccessfully) to incorporate Western tax concepts in the post-1990 era. By implication, a greater awareness of tax culture could avoid these problems.

Nerré's focus is more theoretical than the approach in this book, and he is understandably more focused on European than American tax policy. But his work is both thoughtful and sophisticated, and constitutes probably the most comprehensive effort at developing a comprehensive theory of tax culture to date. We shall have occasion to refer to it in Chapter 3.[22]

21 See, e.g., Anders Stridh & Lennart Wittberg, *From Feared Tax Collector to Popular Service Agency* (Stockholm: Skatteverket (Swedish Tax Authority), 2015).

22 The most comprehensive statement of his theory is probably Birger Nerré, "The Concept of Tax Culture," *National Tax Journal*, 94 (2001), 288–95.

## 2.6 TAX CULTURE AND POPULAR ATTITUDES: "INDIVIDUALIST" AND "COLLECTIVIST" SOCIETIES

Tax culture is expressed on an individual level by a taxpayer's response to her own taxpaying obligations. On a more collective level, it may find expression in popular attitudes toward tax-related issues, such as the appropriate level of taxation, the proper mix of taxes (income, excise, value added, etc.), and attitudes toward tax evasion or avoidance by businesses and individuals. The two sets of attitudes are closely related, in that an individual who was (say) politically hostile to progressive income taxation might also be unenthusiastic about paying her own income taxes; but they remain conceptually distinct.

This broader, collective concept of tax culture has likewise been the subject of considerable scholarly attention. In a series of books and articles Marjorie Kornhauser has evaluated American attitudes toward money, wealth, and inequality and their implications for a wide variety of tax issues, over a period ranging from World War I until the early twenty-first century. Not surprisingly, Kornhauser has found these attitudes to be conflicted, with resentment toward wealthy plutocrats balanced by respect and even admiration for their initiative and accomplishments on the part of more successful taxpayers.[23]

One of Kornhauser's most interesting observations regards the cyclical nature of tax attitudes. For example, she found that arguments against progressive taxation in the 1920s were almost indistinguishable from those of the 1980s and thereafter, and the responses to them were remarkably similar as well. Much of the history of American tax policy can, per Kornhauser, be explained by the alternation of these attitudes.[24]

On a more abstract level, Edward McCaffery has critiqued the values and procedures that underlie the American approach to taxation, which he finds lags behind attitudes and behaviors in other fields. This is particularly true with respect to women and families, the taxation of which are the subject of McCaffery's best-known book.[25] Thus, many tax concepts remain stuck in an earlier era even when popular attitudes have long since moved on. (I frequently tell my own class that if they want to understand the world of the tax code – a solid distinction between single and married couples, a sharp line between business and personal life, and so forth – they should watch "Leave it to Beaver" or other 1960s-era TV sitcoms.)

Assaf Likhovski's work considers tax culture in both its narrower and broader forms. In a 2004 article "The Duke and the Lady," Likhovski considers judicial responses to tax avoidance in the United States and United Kingdom before World War II, concluding that law, philosophy, and morality as well as purely economic

23 See Marjorie E. Kornhauser, "The Morality of Money: American Attitudes Toward Wealth and the Income Tax," 70 *Indiana Law Review*, (1994), 119.

24 Ibid.

25 See Edward J. McCaffery, *Taxing Women* (Chicago and London: University of Chicago Press, 1997).

factors are important in understanding the two countries' divergent judicial decisions.

In another article, "Is Tax Law Culturally Specific? Lessons From the History of Income Tax Law in Mandatory Palestine,"[26] Likhovski expands his analysis to the entire tax system of his home country, which was essentially imported by the British to wartime Palestine in 1941. One of Likhovski's key insights is that rules identical on paper may have very different significance when applied in a different political and cultural context. For example, the colonial tax system – while purportedly neutral as between Jews and Arabs – had the effect of bringing many more Jews than Arabs into the tax system, with important implications for the fiscal stability of the Jewish and Arab entities after the British departed.

A cultural analysis has also been applied to narrower issues, including Joseph Bankman's work on American tax shelters and Robert Clark's classic article on the culture of tax lawyers, alluded to above.[27] (The latter in particular was something of a cult classic among tax students in the late 1970s.) The concept of subcultures, which may be as broad as an ethnic group or as narrow as a single law firm, is once again of importance here.

While the body of work reviewed in the preceding passages is useful, it suggests a number of problems. The first is a question of definition. Unless they are tax professionals, most people do not draw a clear line between their attitude toward tax issues and their broader political outlook. For example, someone who supports or opposes progressive income taxation may do so because they like (or dislike) government spending rather than because of any particular tax philosophy. People's attitudes may also be inconsistent or cyclical in nature, supporting taxes when they like the government in question and opposing them when they do not. For example, many Americans resist federal taxes, but are less hostile to state and local taxes that they feel contribute more directly to their communities. These factors, together with the technical limitations of survey research, make it difficult to determine people's "real" or inherent tax attitudes, or if these even exist.

A second, related problem concerns the relationship between ordinary citizens and tax elites. With the exception of their own tax returns, ordinary people influence tax policy only indirectly, by participating in elections, contributing to political campaigns, or expressing their opinions in popular forums (such as newspapers, television, or social media). If they feel strongly enough, they may participate in taxpayer organizations or tax-related lobbying groups, although the latter affect outcomes only indirectly. Typically these organizations limit themselves to general themes (lower taxes, more equitable tax principles, etc.) or the issues affecting a particular industry that the individual is somehow connected with.

26 11 "Theoretical Inquiries in Law," (2010) 725. Likhovski's work is discussed further in Chapter 6.

27 Clark, *The Morphogenesis of Subchapter C*, 6; Joseph A. Bankman, "The New Market in Corporate Tax Shelters," 83 *Tax Notes* (1999) 1775.

Not surprisingly, then, most work on "tax culture" – when not devoted to purely compliance issues – actually concerns the attitudes and behavior of a relatively small elite, including lawyers, economists, and assorted bureaucrats, who participate in the creation and execution of tax policy. The works of McCaffery, Likhovski, and to some extent even Kornhauser are largely in this category. The same is true for the more focused work of Clark, Bankman, and other tax and business law scholars. There is nothing necessarily wrong with this: public policy always reflects the interaction of elite and mass, and the term "culture" itself can mean either sophisticated or mass tastes.[28] But it does suggest the importance of specifying exactly whose attitudes we are interested in and precisely what culture, or subculture, is being described in any particular instance.

Finally, broader tax preferences may be shaped by institutions as well as shaping them. Thus, as McCaffery or Kornhauser would surely agree, the US tax code tells a story about the distinctions between men and women, rich and poor, and business and personal expenditures as well as reflecting the story that is told to it by taxpayers. Tax attitudes are inevitably a reflection of this story as well as being reflected in it. The differing effects of the income tax in mandatory Palestine were a reflection of structural differences between the Jewish and Arab communities as much as or more than individual attitudes. There is a sort of "chicken and egg" problem, since attitudes affect institutions but are themselves shaped or even created by their existing institutional setting. This is simply a tax version of the broader attitudes versus institutions conundrum: where, precisely, is the student of "culture" to begin?

My own work on progressive taxation provided a rude introduction to this phenomenon. Somewhat naively, I expected that progressivity or regressivity would reflect deeply held popular attitudes in each of the countries that I studied. Instead, I found popular attitudes were elusive and, when they could be determined, political structures were frequently of much greater importance.[29] For example, Italian tax attitudes were closely tied to the left-right political divide and (more recently) the influence of the European Union, while Israeli tax policy was in many cases inherited from the British rather than reflecting any Israeli values at all. American tax attitudes frequently had little to with taxes themselves, instead reflecting spending priorities or the different levels of government (state, federal, and local) to which taxes were paid. Chinese tax officials repeatedly discussed "harmony" as an argument for progressive taxation, but whether this was a popular value or simply a current propaganda theme was difficult to determine. Scandinavia had high, albeit not necessarily progressive, taxes on individuals but less so on corporations: no one was particularly bothered.[30]

28 See the alternate definitions of culture cited in Chapter 1.

29 The progressivity issue is discussed further in Chapter 5.

30 Michael A. Livingston, "From Milan to Mumbai, Changing in Tel Aviv: Reflections on Progressive Taxation and 'Progressive' Politics in a Globalized but Still Local World," *American Journal of Comparative Law*, 54 (1996), 555; Michael A. Livingston, "From Mumbai to Shanghai, with a Side

None of this means that attitudes are unimportant, or that they don't vary significantly across different countries. But they are only one part of the overall equation, and institutions remain important in shaping popular attitudes and in determining how they are translated into real-world policy decisions. In some cases, these institutions reflect the attitudes and values of foreign of colonial powers rather than those of the country that they are serving. All of these points would be second nature to a good social scientist, but they can be easy to overlook in a tax context. (The role of tax institutions is considered further in Chapter 3.)

## 2.7 HOW DEEP IS YOUR CULTURE? THE QUESTION OF HISTORICAL CONTINGENCY

Institutions, then, affect popular attitudes as well as being affected by them. But institutions themselves are not static, instead reflecting political and economic changes in the society in question. Sometimes these changes are incremental, as with the development of American tax policy norms since the 1950s. At times they may be more radical or even violent in nature: ask anyone who lived through the past half-century in Moscow, Budapest, or Berlin. While changes sometimes arise organically within a society, in other cases they are provoked by outside events or intervention, as in the case of a war, invasion, or large-scale changes in the international environment.

The phenomenon discussed above suggests that, together with attitudes and institutions, the matter of historical context or contingency must be taken into account in evaluating tax (or other) culture. This may include broad-based changes, like the British Empire or the Russian Revolution, or narrower developments, like the drafting of a new tax code. Because tax is often perceived as a technical area and allowed to "slip under the radar," historical developments that are otherwise long forgotten sometimes continue to shape tax policy in surprising and important ways. At times, events forgotten in their country of origin may have a significant effect in a different location, as we shall observe below.

Perhaps the most sophisticated student of historical contingency in tax policy is Sven Steinmo, an American political scientist who has written extensively on comparative fiscal issues. In *Taxation and Democracy: Swedish, British and American Approaches to Financing the Modern State*,[31] Steinmo notes that tax patterns in the three countries studied – high but not especially progressive taxes in Sweden, superficially progressive taxes but with numerous subsidies and loopholes in the United States, and an oscillation between higher and lower rates in the United Kingdom – have little if anything to do with the values of the people who live in the relevant countries. But they have everything to do with governmental

Trip to Hong Kong: China, India, and The Future of Progressive Taxation in an Asian-Led World," *Theoretical Inquiries in Law*, 11 (2010), 539. Scandinavian taxes are analyzed in Chapter 3.

[31] New Haven: Yale University Press, 1993.

structure and decision-making, specifically, the tax legislative process and the role of interest groups in influencing that process. For example, the American and British systems differ less because of divergent ideologies than because the American government frequently lacks a congressional majority, requiring it to give away various tax favors in order to pass a tax bill. The Swedish system, in turn, reflects the needs of the domestic welfare state balanced with the importance of export promotion in what remains a relatively small if prosperous country.

Still more interesting is Steinmo's analysis of historical factors – what he calls contingencies, and what we have referred to earlier as "quirks" – that may have little connection to current political and economic realities. For example, the Swedish tax and welfare system dates from a compromise between business and labor leaders reached at a resort near Stockholm in the 1930s: had the economy not been concentrated in the hands of a very small number of people – or had the pressure from Nazi Germany and Soviet Russia not been so great – the system might have developed in a wholly different manner. Japanese fiscal policy reflects a consensus among essentially paternalistic public and private actors, a system developed in the early postwar era that almost everyone agrees is inefficient, but which persists anyway because it is so deeply embedded in the country's political and economic institutions.

In a subsequent book[32] Steinmo develops his argument further, suggesting that national systems undergo "evolution" in a manner not wholly dissimilar from living beings, with unpredictable or random changes – something like evolutive mutations – assuming significant importance and prior decisions constraining the choices that are available to later generations, whether they have agreed to them or not. Put more bluntly, countries often find themselves "stuck" with institutional arrangements that may have little to do with what they would agree to under conditions of free choice. A similar analysis applies not only to tax systems but to the overall political, economic, and social structures of the nations involved.

Steinmo's analysis is highly persuasive and accounts for an apparent anomaly in comparative tax studies, namely, the frequent disconnect between a country's tax policy and its broader cultural norms. I would add only two observations to Steinmo's theory. First, historical quirks or contingencies may result not only from differences in overall political structure, but from narrower differences that affect specific institutions or actors. For example, American tax policy was for decades heavily influenced by two nonpartisan bodies, the Joint Committee on Taxation (legislative branch) and the Treasury Department Office of Tax Legislative Counsel (executive branch), although the influence of the former appears to have waned somewhat in recent years. Italian capital gain taxation is shaped in part by the fact that the country's major commercial center (Milan) happens to be located only

[32] Sven Steinmo, *The Evolution of Modern States: Sweden, Japan and the United States* (Cambridge University Press, 2010).

an hour or two from Switzerland, historically the world's premier tax haven. I don't think either of these situations reflects any truly profound development in American or Italian history: they are simply things that happened for unrelated reasons and that, once present, had to be dealt with by policy-makers. Similar quirks affect other countries.

Second, tax ideas and institutions frequently cross national borders because of wars, colonialism, or voluntary borrowing. For example, the Nordic countries have a long history of cooperation in tax matters, so that developments in (say) Sweden may spread seamlessly to Denmark or Norway without the population of the latter two countries even being aware of it. The entire tax systems of Israel, India, and several other countries were originally drafted in London, while that of Japan dates from the Shoup Report, which was written by American bureaucrats in the 1940s. In these and other cases, the tax culture or subculture of a country may (to follow Steinmo's analogy) take on a life of its own, never completely separate from the country's underlying political structure, but never really part of it either.

My personal favorite quirk relates to Indian taxation and reflects a combination of the two phenomena above. It seems that agricultural production in India is historically taxable by state (provincial) governments rather than the Union government, an arrangement that affords enormous tax shelter opportunities and has proved remarkably resilient to change. Why is this the case? Because someone in the British colonial administration decided it, and it became a part of the Indian tax structure that everyone more or less accepted. But of course, in a country where more than half the population works in agriculture, this quirk has enormous influence on tax policy and administration. It did not take very long for tax advisors to devise schemes whereby "urban" income was transferred to "rural" or agricultural zones, thereby avoiding federal tax. A significant amount of administrative effort was then required in order to combat such schemes. At last glance this odd rule continues in effect, albeit subject to a partial integration system that somewhat restricts its tax shelter potential with respect to wealthier taxpayers.[33]

A similar anomaly affects Israel, which didn't even try to tax overseas income until decades after statehood, and for many years had a diffident attitude toward capital gain as well. It seems unlikely that these exemptions derived from deeply held cultural values; indeed, the country was nominally socialist for most of this period, and Menachem Begin (elected 1977) was the first prime minister even to wear a tie in public. Instead, as in India, the relevant practices were inherited from the British colonial (mandate) administration, which found it easiest to level taxes on wage incomes and to forget to a large extent about the rest.[34] The US tax system likewise features several historical contingencies, such as the practice of leaving sales and

33 The gist appears to be that agricultural income remains exempt but is included in computing tax for overall (that is, nonagricultural) income, with an exemption of up to 5,000 rupees. See generally http://incometaxindia.gov.in/tutorials/11.tax%20free%20incomes%20final.pdf

34 The Israeli tax system is discussed further in Chapter 5.

property taxation to states and localities, even though most countries tax the former (and sometimes the latter) at the national level.[35] While this practice is tied to federalism, the latter does not tell you what taxes to impose at what levels: it just happened that way, for historical or political reasons. The use of real property taxes to finance public schools, another American tradition, is similarly quirky and perhaps even illogical in nature: I am aware of no other country that does this in quite the same way.

The arrangements above may be said to be "cultural" in nature, in the sense that they form part of the accepted beliefs and practices of tax professionals in a given society, but it is hard to connect them to broader societal values or attitudes in any meaningful sense. To cite Primo Levi, they are something like the inclusion of inert compounds in a chemical formula, or the habit of buttoning men's shirts on the right-hand side and women's on the left: inherited practices that become part of the warp and woof of a given industry's practice but cannot easily be explained or rationalized to someone outside the industry.[36] Whether or not to label them cultural thus seems arbitrary at best. For the moment, it seems best to place them in a separate category of historical quirks or contingencies and leave it at that.

## 2.8 ATTITUDES AND INSTITUTIONS: THE TWIN PILLARS OF TAX CULTURE

The discussion above suggests that tax attitudes differ substantially both between and within different countries. But it also suggests that there is no straight line between attitudes and outcomes, because tax attitudes are frequently inchoate in nature; because they may be difficult to separate from attitudes toward other, nontax policy issues; and because they are filtered through elites of one kind or another rather than expressing themselves in an inevitable or direct fashion. Attitudes and behaviors are likewise shaped by political and historical events as well as shaping those events in turn. Sometimes they are dependent upon historical quirks or contingencies that refuse to follow any particular pattern at all.

At the risk of repetition, none of the above would surprise a professional or even an amateur anthropologist terribly much. It is really just another way of saying that attitudes matter, but institutions matter as much or more so, and history sometimes matters the most of all. It is to the question of tax institutions and their development that we now turn.

35 The European VAT is comparable to a sales tax for this purpose.

36 The analogy is derived from Primo Levi, *The Periodic Table* (New York: Schocken Books, 1984).

# 3

# Tax Sociology: The Significance of Tax Institutions

If attitudes form the foundation of tax culture, institutions form its structure. Indeed, a tax itself is a sort of institution, which is created by other institutions (primarily legislatures) and, in turn, requires further institutions to enforce and monitor it. As observed in Chapter 1, institutions are created in response to popular attitudes and, in turn, mold those attitudes, so that it is sometimes hard to determine where one ends and the other begins.

This chapter considers tax institutions and their role in the making and functioning of tax policy. Among the institutions considered are legislatures and other lawmaking bodies; tax administrations; tax-related professions (lawyers, economists, accountants, etc.); and tax education, of both the formal and informal variety. All these institutions are present in all countries, but they function quite differently in them, and the boundaries between them vary significantly in different national settings. While the emphasis is on national tax institutions, the chapter will also discuss supranational organizations, like the European Union and WTO, together with private actors (for example, international LL.M. programs) that have an influence on tax policy.

As in Chapter 1 the emphasis is on constructing a universal, or as universal as possible, model of tax culture rather than describing the culture of any particular country. However, to give some idea of where we are headed, the chapter will conclude with a very brief survey of tax culture in two places, the United States and the Nordic countries, describing some of the basic institutions, attitudes, and historical circumstances that distinguish these two places from each other and from other tax cultures. Chapters 5 and 6 will then apply a similar analysis to a number of different countries and to a number of problems arising in these countries and the global tax system.

For convenience's sake, I will sometimes refer to institutional concerns as "tax sociology" and attitudinal issues, like those in Chapter 1, as "tax anthropology." This is an arbitrary and perhaps invalid distinction as both subjects are part of tax culture and, properly speaking, overlap the two fields. Still, it may be worth a brief detour regarding sociology and its distinct contribution to tax issues.

## 3.1 TAX SOCIOLOGY: A LITTLE BACKGROUND

Sociology has been defined as "the science of society, social institutions, and social relationships." An alternate definition is "the scientific analysis of a social institution as a functioning whole and as it relates to the rest of society."[1] The pioneers of modern sociology include Emile Durkheim, Max Weber, and Karl Marx, each of whom tried to substitute a scientific, empirical study of human relations for what had previously been a largely normative discipline. As compared to anthropology, sociology tends to emphasize institutions rather than individuals and modern rather than primitive societies, although there is a substantial overlap.

Law and sociology is somewhat more developed than its anthropological cousin, although it does not always bother to employ the sociology label. Thus Marxism, which is explicit in some legal scholarship and implicit in other work (notably the Critical Legal Studies movement), is essentially a form of sociology, although its founder has also been claimed by economics, philosophy, and various other disciplines. Feminist jurisprudence likewise owes a heavy debt to sociological theory and method. Legal positivism and the so-called functional method, as discussed in Chapter 2, owe a heavy debt to Durkheim, while the study of institutions and professions proceeds, in part, from the scholarship of Durkheim and (later) of Michel Foucault, a French philosopher whose work crossed the boundary of several different fields.

Moving back somewhat in time, observations like those of Kornhauser and Mehrotra regarding the impact of religion on tax policy call to mind the work of Max Weber on the "Protestant ethic" and its impact on the development of capitalism.[2] Indeed, any attempt to study "Law and Society," as a popular North American conference is labeled, inevitably invokes a measure of sociology whether or not the participants refer formally to the latter. Law and sociology appears to be especially advanced in the United Kingdom, going by the somewhat infelicitous name "socio-legal studies," but there are numerous North American participants, as well.

Tax or (as it is frequently called) fiscal sociology has produced a variety of studies, many of them by academic lawyers rather than sociologists. Some of this work has been historical in nature, attempting to explain why tax systems developed in a particular way and why outcomes in one place differ from those in another. A good example is the work of Ajay Mehrotra, who has both edited a recent collection on "the new fiscal sociology" and produced a separate, independent work on the historical origins of progressive taxation in the United States.[3] Mehtrotra's work is especially interesting for emphasizing the relationship between

[1] See www.merriam-webster.com/dictionary/sociology. The same dictionary defines anthropology as "the study of human beings ... through time and space and in relation to physical character, environmental and social relations, and culture."

[2] Max Weber, *The Protestant Ethic and the Spirit of Capitalism* (1904).

[3] A. Mehotra, I. W. Martin, & M. Prasad (eds.), *The New Fiscal Sociology: Taxation in Comparative and Historical Perspective* (Cambridge University Press, 2009); Ajay Mehtotra, *Making the Modern*

tax policy and developments in the broader culture, including politics, religion, and social life, rather than treating tax as a self-contained subject. The work of Isaac William Martin and Monica Prasad, who studied the French and American tax systems as well as coediting the collection above, is also worthy of mention. Both Martin and Prasad are professional sociologists who see tax policy as a reflection of political, social, and even religious rather than purely economic factors.[4]

Edward McCaffery, a law professor, and Sven Steinmo, a political scientist, have also written extensively on the subject of tax institutions and their impact on substantive tax policy outcomes. Indeed, it was the divergence between the tax institutions of different countries that led Steinmo to his theory of the evolution of tax systems, discussed in Chapter 2. McCaffery's work ranges from the taxation of women to the significance of behavioral economics for tax policy, a subject he has revisited several times.[5]

The nascent field of critical tax studies, with its emphasis on the political assumptions underlying tax law, has likewise produced several useful studies, notably on tax rules affecting women, minorities, and LGBTQ taxpayers.[6] The social and cultural implications of purportedly "neutral" tax rules, like joint tax returns or the distinction between business and personal expenses, are a particular target of this work. The boundaries between fields are especially fluid here, with sociology, anthropology, and political science overlapping with each other and with traditional legal studies: the difference is one of emphasis rather than kind.

One limitation of sociological studies is that they tend to involve a small number of countries and, almost inevitably, tend to identify broad differences between societies and institutions as explaining specific legal or policy outcomes. The role of historical factors, foreign imports, and simple quirks in the making and enforcement of tax law may sometimes accordingly be overlooked. (This is perhaps one reason why collaborative studies between sociologists and law professors, who tend to thrive on details, have been so popular.) None of this is intended to take away from the field, but rather to suggest that a certain skepticism is in order regarding the ability of any individual theory to explain all relevant tax outcomes.

## 3.2 TAX LAWMAKING AND THE TAX LEGISLATIVE PROCESS

The first element to consider in constructing a comprehensive tax sociology is how tax laws are made. In some respects this is easier for tax than for other areas of law. In

*American Fiscal State: Law, Politics, and the Rise of Progressive Taxation, 1877–1929* (Cambridge University Press, 2014).

4 See, e.g., I. W. Martin & M. Prasad, "Taxes and Fiscal Sociology," *Annual Review of Sociology*, 40 (1996), 341–55.

5 See Edward McCaffery, *Taxing Women* (University of Chicago Press, 1997); Edward McCaffery & Joel Slemrod (eds.), *Behavioral Public Finance* (New York: Russell Sage Press, 2006).

6 See Bridget J. Crawford & Anthony Infanti, *Critical Tax Theory: An Introduction* (Cambridge University Press, 2009).

many areas there is a longstanding debate between positivists, who see law as created by the sovereign, and advocates of natural law, who trace it to timeless principles created by nature or (in some cases) by God. Indeed the debate between positivism and natural law is among the most famous in legal theory.[7]

In tax law the positivists reign more or less supreme. The income tax is a couple of hundred years old in the United Kingdom, barely a hundred in the United States, and less than that in most other places. Excise and property taxes are older – the tithe is biblical in origin – but they are less important and current versions bear little if any resemblance to the earlier texts. No one seriously argues that section 368 was handed down on Mount Sinai or depreciation was preached in the Gospels.

With its emphasis on functional lawmaking, positivism focuses attention on variations in the legislative process among different societies. These differences involve various factors, including the actors in the process; the procedure by which the laws are enacted; and the balance between national and supranational forces. This last item is easily overlooked by Americans, who assume their independence in tax matters and (if they are really honest with themselves) their ability to dictate to other countries, with the possible exception of China, as well. But for many nations the actions of supranational bodies (EU, IMF, etc.), or simply of larger and more powerful countries, are the starting point for their own tax legislation. It is probably not an exaggeration to say that only two countries (the United States and China) can claim something approaching full sovereignty in tax matters, and even they are more constricted than they sometimes like to believe that they are, as we shall observe below.

The issue of domestic actors and processes is likewise more complicated than at first glance. On a superficial level these may appear to be similar everywhere. Every country has some kind of legislature than enacts tax laws together with an executive that enforces them and a judiciary that interprets them in borderline cases. These functions remain distinct, even if the institutions that carry them out may not always be.

The differences come in the structure of institutions and the rules by which they function. These are frequently quite different even in otherwise similar countries. Thus, in the United Kingdom or Canada, the executive is chosen from the majority party in the legislature, with the result that – barring extreme controversy – the government's proposals are likely to be enacted with relatively minor changes. Attention thus naturally focuses on the government's tax program rather than the attitudes or beliefs of individual legislators. By contrast, in the United States, the Congress will frequently amend the executive's proposals or, in some cases, simply throw them away and start over again. (The current Congress is unlikely even to read them.) The extent of judicial authority in taxation is likewise quite different in these countries, with American courts asserting an ability to interpret or simply create new tax law that would seem unusual in other English-speaking countries.

7 See Chapter 2.

The differences in legislative process are still greater between civil and common law countries, or between democracies and authoritarian nations. In the latter, it goes without saying that the government's, meaning essentially the executive's, proposals are likely to become law in all or most cases. With respect to civil law countries, the legislature retains lawmaking powers but the style of tax and other laws is likely to be quite different than in common law jurisdictions. For example, the Italian tax code – like the country's civil, criminal, or other codifications – is as a general rule more detailed and systematic than that in the United States or other English-speaking jurisdictions.

The differences above are generic in nature, applying to the legislative process in general. But there are other, more tax-specific differences. There is a perception in many countries that tax law is more technical, and perhaps more important for government finances, than other areas of law. Because of this perception – or simply for historical reasons – these countries allocate tax legislative power in a manner that is different from other policy areas. This procedural difference has important implications for substantive outcomes.

China provides an interesting example. An authoritarian country with a strong Confucian tradition, China vests a great deal of lawmaking authority in the executive/administrative branch and relatively little in the courts and the nominal legislature. This tradition is particularly strong in taxation, which is classified as a division of finance rather than law. Thus accounting firms have far more influence than law firms, and issues that would be considered "legal" in other countries tend to be classified as essentially administrative in nature. The State Administration of Taxation (SAT), which occupies large and rather forbidding offices in an outlying district of Beijing, is accordingly the principal player in tax rule-making and what Americans would call tax litigation. Tax legislation itself tends to be rather general in nature, and the role of the courts is with some exceptions rather limited.

The Chinese question highlights a more general problem, namely, the question of professional expertise in taxation. As noted above, there is a frequent sense that tax issues are either too hard or too important to be left to mere politics. We thus have the phenomenon of the "neutral" or "apolitical" tax expert, as represented by bodies like the Congressional Joint Committee on Taxation and the Treasury Department Office of Tax Analysis in the United States and similar bodies in other nations. While these bodies exist partially to provide professional economic analysis, they frequently include lawyers as well as economists and are expected to provide advice on substantive matters of tax policy as well as technical support.

The apolitical character of these bodies is, of course, something of a myth, as the often bitter disputes over revenue estimates in the United States indicate, but they retain a significant if often contested authority that has no precise parallel in nontax matters. Interestingly, the concept of neutral or professional tax staffs crosses the line between civil and common law and even between democratic and authoritarian countries, as does the tendency to compartmentalize tax and spending functions, although these are closely related, and it may be difficult to evaluate one independently of the other. This is not to say that the difference between democratic and authoritarian societies is irrelevant, but rather that there is a certain authoritarian tendency in tax matters in all countries: the question is one of degree and balance rather than of invariable essence.

## 3.3 TAX ENFORCEMENT AND TAX ADMINISTRATION

If legislation provides the essential structure of tax law, it is tax administration that puts meat on the bones. Administration and enforcement are so central to tax law that people often assume it is the only source of law: law students frequently refer to "the IRS code" and taxpayers will say that "I owe money to the IRS" rather than to the government as a whole. These statements are factually incorrect, but not by much: tax laws are typically so general in nature, and litigation so rare, that administrators are often the primary and sometimes the only source of authority in a given area. Even tax "casebooks" make frequent reference to administrative decisions.

Every country has some form of tax administration, but they differ substantially in organization, staffing, and institutional culture. There are also significant variations in the allocation of power between the tax administration and other institutions, including the treasury or finance ministry (department) and the enacting legislature itself. For convenience, it may be useful to consider these issues one at a time.

A first question relates to organizational structure. In some countries the tax administration is part of a larger government ministry – typically the finance or treasury department – while in others it is an independent body. In some countries it has responsibility for proposing tax legislation, while in others it is limited to enforcing the laws already passed. The United States has a hybrid system in which the IRS is nominally part of the Treasury Department but functions more or less independently. For example, the drafting of regulations is directed by the Treasury with substantial IRS input, while revenue rulings and procedures, together with private "letter rulings," are issued by the IRS. In some countries the tax administration is less independent than in the United States, although in others it is more so. Like the question of apolitical tax experts, the issue of tax autonomy is related to, but distinct from, the question of governmental form: some countries that are rather nondemocratic in nature nonetheless have a relatively independent tax administration, while some more democratic countries have a less independent one, and so forth.

A second question relates to qualification and staffing. In some countries the tax administration is dominated by economists, while in other countries lawyers or (less frequently) accountants play a central role. In some countries it is dominated by lifetime civil servants, while in others there is a fair amount of movement between the public and private sectors. These differences once again cut across political categories. For example, the United States assigns a relatively prominent role to lawyers in tax administration, while both China and India, notwithstanding vastly different political systems, assign them a much smaller role. Several European countries, notwithstanding their highly developed and prestigious legal professions, do the same. To some extent, these differences reflect differences in the structure and function of the tax-related professions, as discussed in Section 4.

Finally – at the risk of some repetition – there is what might be called the institutional culture of tax administration, that is, the values and attitudes that tax administrators bring to their role and how these values and attitudes are, in turn, shaped by the institutions of which they are a part. An important if elusive question is how tax administrators understand their function: is it primarily to enforce the laws as enacted, or to raise the maximum amount of money possible with the available institutional resources? Do they see themselves as advocates for taxpayers, as the government's first line of defense against them, or some combination of the two? (This issue will be addressed further in the discussion of American and Nordic tax administration.)

The question of tax administration is closely related to the issue of tax legislation and, in a broader sense, to the attitudinal issues addressed in Chapter 2. To the extent that the legislature takes an assertive role in tax lawmaking, the administration is likely to be circumscribed in its range of possible interpretations, and to understand its function as achieving the goals of the legislature rather than mere revenue-raising. If ordinary citizens have a more positive attitude toward tax compliance, the tax administration is likely to view them through a less oppositional lens, and vice-versa. Either a vicious circle of tax avoidance and confrontational administration, or a more virtuous cycle of compliance and cooperation, are likely to be self-reinforcing. These should accordingly be seen as interdependent items rather than as separate, freestanding issues.

## 3.4 TAX LITIGATION AND THE RESOLUTION OF TAX DISPUTES

In any tax system there will be certain disputes that either cannot be resolved by legislation or administration, or that arise after those processes are completed. We usually think of these as judicial disputes, although (as in China) they may not always be handled by a separate branch of government. Because disputed issues tend to be difficult ones, the dispute resolution function – even when it occupies relatively limited resources – may be disproportionately significant for the development of tax law.

The resolution of tax disputes may be handled in several ways. A key distinction is between courts of general jurisdiction, which handle tax matters as one of several subject areas, and specialized tax courts, which handle taxation or fiscal matters exclusively. The United States is once again a sort of hybrid here, having a specialized Tax Court which handles most but not all trial-level tax cases, but whose decisions are appealable to the regular Court of Appeal and (ultimately) to the Supreme Court. (Tax cases may also be brought in the regular District Courts or the United States Claims Court, which are appealable to essentially the same places.) Although it is in theory more expert than other courts, the Tax Court has never really been especially prestigious in nature, a situation which may result from the (rather politicized) method of choosing its judges.

Other countries offer a range of different solutions. Thus Italy has specialized tax courts, but France does not, although their legal systems are in many other respects similar. The constitutional courts in both these countries as well as in Germany have also made several decisions with important tax effects, although these in theory flow from their constitutional rather than tax-specific jurisdiction. For example, the French Constitutional Council struck down a special tax on high incomes, while the Italian Constitutional Court held that joint returns on married couples violated each individual's right to be taxed solely on their own income. (It is difficult to imagine the US Supreme Court making quite this broad a holding, although perhaps not quite impossible.)

Some countries make use of administrative tribunals that have an essentially judicial function, although they are constitutionally speaking part of the executive branch. Indeed, the US Tax Court, which used to be called the Board of Tax Appeals, is nominally in this category, a so-called Article One rather than Article Three court. The decisions of these tribunals are usually, although not always, appealable to the judicial branch. The number of tax cases actually accepted by the courts and the standard for overturning an administrative decision likewise vary between countries.

The role of tax adjudication is, not surprisingly, tied to the more general question of judicial power and authority. In common law jurisdictions like the United States, courts often assert a broad authority to make law even when the tax itself is statutory in origin. Thus, the US Supreme Court has articulated a variety of concepts, including the business purpose rule for corporate acquisitions and the very definition of income under section 61, that have little or no basis in the statute.

In theory, the courts in civil law systems, which are statute- or code-based, would take a more skeptical view of judicial lawmaking. But this difference is sometimes honored in the breach, as tax issues become more complicated and problems arise that were not contemplated in the original legislation. The concept of judicial review in constitutional cases, which spread from the United States to other countries, further complicates the equation: it is not unusual for constitutional courts to strike down specific provisions or even entire pieces of legislation, making them in some cases more important than the country's nominal tax tribunals. The decisions of the French and Italian constitutional courts, cited above, are only one example of this process.

Together with the issue of judicial philosophy one must consider the matter of judicial attitudes. There is a sense in some countries that judges do not like tax cases and do their best to avoid them. One story, perhaps apocryphal, tells of a US Supreme Court Justice who was asked why he sang so loudly at the Chief Justice's Christmas Party. "Because otherwise he gives me all the tax cases," the justice responded. An obvious answer is to create a separate court of tax appeals, but it is not clear that this would result in better or more consistent jurisprudence. There is also a fear that a separate tax court might be insensitive to nontax concerns, or create precedents for the use of legislative history and so forth that would then carry over to other areas.

The use of specialized courts, like the creation of specialized tax agencies, raises again the question of tax uniqueness and the effort to insulate tax policy from broader political and judicial processes. But it also demonstrates the limitations of that effort. Even when specialized bodies exist, they typically report to organizations that are closer to the political or judicial mainstream and that follow procedural and substantive norms that originate outside the tax system. The very structure of the tax laws frequently reflects concepts like common law, civil law, or judicial (constitutional) review that are essentially nontax in origin. All this is merely another way of saying that tax culture is never entirely self-sufficient, but rather forms part of the broader legal, administrative, and political culture in the country in question and is subject to similar pressures.

## 3.5 TAX EDUCATION AND THE TAX PROFESSIONS

Because the income tax is relatively recent, it largely attached itself to existing professions – lawyer, accountant, economist – rather than creating a new one. Thus, while there is often a tax collector, and the tax administration is sometimes called "the taxman," there is no such thing as a taxologist or a taxolog, although there are many tax lawyers, tax economists, tax accountants, etc.[8] This is an important point, because there is a significant difference in perspective between these professions, and which of them predominates has a substantial influence on a country's tax culture.

In North American circles it is common to think of lawyers and economists as dominant and roughly equal players, with accountants in a supporting role and others more or less irrelevant to day-to-day tax practice. When I worked at the Joint Tax Committee we had roughly equal numbers of the first two categories, and a handful of the second. I don't recall a staff anthropologist, although perhaps we could have used one.

[8] This is perhaps an oversimplification: tax collector or tax preparer – even at one point "tax farmer" – has constituted a separate profession, albeit not always an especially honored one. In today's world, however – at the very least in more "advanced" countries – these have given way to subdivisions of wider professions as described in the text.

From a global perspective, this situation is actually somewhat uncommon. In most countries lawyers play a marginal role in tax policy, although they are often indispensable to individual people with specific tax problems. We have already observed this situation in China, where economists and other nonlawyers dominate tax policy and accounting firms are more influential than law firms at the private level. But this is also true in many European countries, where lawyers and law professors tend to be occupied with doctrinal questions and the "big picture" issues of tax policy – who should be taxed at what rates and subject to what deductions, exclusions, etc. – are left largely to others. In India a good deal of tax lawyers' time appears to be devoted to litigation regarding the deductibility of chauffeurs and other personal assistants; at most law faculties tax is not even a regular course.

The significance of professional cultures can hardly be overstated. Lawyers and economists have radically different training, the former emphasizing the resolution of individual disputes and the latter the allocation of resources in the broader society. This also means that lawyers' training tends to emphasize fairness ("equity") and economists' efficiency, although there is inevitably some overlap between the two fields. (That is one reason why nondemocratic societies are reluctant to admit a large number of foreign lawyers.) Accountants have a separate culture that stresses still other values, while business consultants, who often give tax advice, present yet another category.

While economics is a universal discipline, legal education varies dramatically in different countries. The most obvious distinction is between common law jurisdictions, which emphasize an inductive method of learning (the so-called case method), and civil law countries, which tend to deduce legal rules from broader, original principles. But there are significant variations within each family: legal education and the legal profession are different in the United States and United Kingdom or France and Germany, not to speak of the differences between Western countries and their non-Western peers.

One interesting way to grasp the difference in tax education is to thumb through an introductory tax textbook in each new country. American tax casebooks are essentially inductive in nature, beginning with cases involving free room and board at a Hawaiian hotel, employers who offer to pay their employees' taxes, or other odd sets of facts from which students are expected to figure out the underlying principles of tax law on their own.[9] This follows the lead of casebooks in other fields, one of whose opening cases, concerning a man whose hand became hairy after a botched skin transplant, was sufficiently entertaining to form the opening scene of a popular movie.[10]

9 This issue was discussed further in Chapter 2.

10 *The Paper Chase* (20th Century Fox, 1973). The film was popular enough to spawn an eponymous TV series.

By contrast, Italian students learn tax law from *manuali* (textbooks) that proceed methodically from one subject to another – what is a tax, who is the taxpayer, etc. – with hardly any case references at all. (Perhaps this is why there are no movies about Italian law schools.)[11] Students brought up in these two systems will obviously approach the same problems in different ways, the Americans tending to begin with the facts and proceed to the relevant law, and the Italians moving intellectually in the opposite direction. Economics textbooks are more similar than the legal variety, but still reflect differences in the culture and experience of the countries that use them.

I witnessed some of the differences in tax thinking when I attended a meeting of the European Association of Tax Law Professors in Paris about a decade ago. An issue arose regarding the right of taxpayers to contest determinations by national tax authorities. Several of the British participants said that the individual taxpayers' rights should come first. But these are the designated tax authorities, responded several continental professors, what right do individuals have to challenge their decisions? I have often felt that the Brexit campaign began at that moment.

The difference between professions, and between professional education in different countries, means that different tax cultures will approach the same problem with fundamentally different mental frameworks and apparatus. To the extent that tax policy emphasizes law rather than economics, these differences are likely to become that much greater. We shall have occasion to revisit this problem in later chapters.

## 3.6 LAWYERS, ACCOUNTANTS, AND THE STRUCTURE OF TAX PRACTICE

Together with the philosophical issues above, one must consider differences in the day-to-day nature of tax practice. How that practice is conducted, and what precisely it consists of, varies significantly between countries.

Because of the technical nature of tax law, there is an inevitable tendency toward specialization, with practitioners who become expert in tax matters tending to spend all or most of their time on them to the exclusion of other subjects. But the level of specialization and the prestige attaching to it each vary substantially. While in some jurisdictions tax is a prestigious specialty that involves a high degree of technical expertise and (not entirely coincidentally) a high degree of remuneration, in others it is more akin to political problem-solving, something like a local real estate lawyer in the United States rather than a federal tax advisor.[12] (This situation also

[11] There is, however, a well-known article about the portrayal of tax lawyers in American popular culture. Paul Caron, "Tax Myopia, or Mama Don't Let Your Babies Grow Up to Be Tax Lawyers," *Virginia Tax Review*, 13 (1994), 517.

[12] I can still remember, as a little boy, my father refusing to leave synagogue until we had shaken hands with a certain prominent member of the congregation. I assume that he was a great scholar or

predominates in state and local tax practice, particularly in smaller jurisdictions.) This distinction, in turn, depends on a combination of factors rather than one single item. While a higher degree of technical complexity sometimes correlates with the size or wealth of a country, in other cases it may depend upon the nature of the tax system and the way in which it allocates decision-making authority: there is no simple rule.

The United States is an extreme of a highly specialized, rule-driven tax culture, with tax experts constituting a self-contained fraternity having more than a little condescension even toward other professionals. The tax code and regulations are highly detailed, and the number of cases, rulings, and so forth is so vast that many salaried practitioners, let alone ordinary taxpayers, are able to access them only by means of some form of electronic intermediary. I personally have spent thirty-five years in the tax field, and until three years ago I was the only person I know to file a tax return in hard copy without using paid tax preparation software. I broke down only after I made a $5,000 federal error and several smaller mistakes on my state tax returns (the period for reassessment is still open).[13]

While the complexity of tax law is universal, there is enormous variation in how countries handle that complexity. Israel, an OECD country with a relatively high per capita income, retains a relatively informal tax culture, with most people's taxes withheld at work and a relative dearth of published guidance on many issues. The lack of written rules means that many small businesses essentially negotiate their payments with the tax department rather than adhering to prescribed rules. A select group of politically connected advisors, known colloquially as "fixers," assist people who run afoul of the tax authorities. Sweden prides itself on the simplicity of its tax forms, about which it is said that anyone can complete on their own, although perhaps at some cost in tax fairness. California, about four times the size of Sweden but in theory a state rather than an independent country, has more complicated forms but offers various forms of free assistance to taxpayers in completing them. Most jurisdictions probably lie somewhere between these extremes.[14]

The number and type of tax professionals also varies significantly between countries. The United States and (to some extent) United Kingdom have a tradition of large law and accounting firms with a very high degree of specialization. In many other countries tax advice is given primarily by individuals or smaller firms. There are also substantial differences in career patterns: spending a few years in

community leader. It turned out he was a lawyer known for his skill in reducing real estate tax assessments.

13 It is possible that I am the problem rather than the complexity of the tax forms. After using the software I continued to make errors, some large and others small, that required a series of amended returns. In theory I would be protected by a country, like Sweden, that assists taxpayers in preparing their returns, but my guess is I would be in trouble there, too. There is only so much you can do to protect people from the consequences of their own carelessness.

14 The US (Federal) Government also offers free assistance through the VITA (Volunteer Income Tax Assistance) and similar programs, albeit on a somewhat less comprehensive basis.

government service and returning to private practice is common in the United States, although perhaps less than it used to be, but is relatively uncommon in many countries. This parallels the situation in other areas of practice, where movement between private practice and government service is relatively rare. For example, in Italy, it is difficult to move even between branches of the procuracy (*magistratura*); moving between government and private practice is almost unheard of.

To some extent, differences in tax practice reflect deeper, underlying differences in tax systems, while to some extent they are a response to economic pressures. For example, the tendency to favor accounting over law firms in China is a direct result of the country's political system and its reluctance to allow foreign lawyers access to the country's judicial system. By contrast, the consolidation of small into large firms and the increased specialization of tax practice reflect economic changes that, to a large degree, cross national borders.

Globalization and the competition that it engenders may also affect the balance between different professions. Large accounting firms are typically international in scope, while law firms were traditionally less so, although this is rapidly changing. Accounting firms also have a reputation – probably deserved – for being more enthusiastic than law firms in the marketing of aggressive, not always terribly substantive tax shelters.

Because of these differences, the growth of international tax shelters has favored the rise of global accounting firms and has forced law firms to increase in size and aggressiveness to compete with them. The Panama Papers scandal, involving tax and financial reporting evasion by clients in several countries, revolved around a single Panamanian law firm, Mossack Fonseca, which became so notorious that its website directed you to a statement defending its behavior.[15] (The firm has since announced that it intends to shut down.) Indeed, the ability of such firms to adopt a coordinated, unified strategy while individual countries must respond separately to the activities of their own citizens is a major factor in the rise of the tax shelter industry, and has increased the pressure for international cooperation in tax matters in order to protect revenues.[16]

## 3.7 TRANSNATIONAL AND SUPRANATIONAL INSTITUTIONS

Tax policy is traditionally approached at a national level, the assumption being that the sovereign (i.e., the national government) can do as it pleases. This assumption was never completely accurate: tax policy-makers were always influenced by events in neighboring countries, especially where cross-border transactions were concerned. Today it is even less true than before. As transactions continue to cross

[15] http://mossfonmedia.com, reached through www.mossfon.com (July 11, 2016).
[16] Transactions like this are central to the OECD's Base Erosion and Profit Shifting (BEPS) program, discussed further in Chapter 5.

national borders and taxpayers become ever more sophisticated at moving income to lower-tax jurisdictions, transnational concerns are an important and sometimes dominant factor in national tax policies. This, in turn, has led to the rise of transnational organizations designed to provide a coordinated response to these problems and (not coincidentally) protect national tax bases from further erosion. While there is a large and growing number of such institutions, their effectiveness varies greatly depending on the issue and region concerned.

The most obvious example of transnational tax cooperation is the European Union, where the question of EU compatibility arises for all significant tax changes. A less obvious but no less important example is provided by many developing nations, whose tax policy is so heavily influenced by the IMF and other international bodies as to render it independent in name only. At the opposite extreme are educational programs run by entities like the NYU, Harvard, or Georgetown Law Schools, which train foreign academics and administrators in "neutral" principles of tax policy which they then apply in their own countries. These organizations have no formal power, but they affect the way tax issues are understood and exercise subtle pressure to conform to established international norms. Institutions like the OECD, which run seminars and publish materials for the use of "advanced" societies in tax and other policy fields, lie somewhere in between. The OECD BEPS (Base Erosion and Profit Shifting) project is a good example of its influence.

The issue of transnational tax institutions and their interaction with national tax policy is discussed further in Chapter 4.

## 3.8 INSTITUTIONAL TRANSPLANTS AND THE TIME LAG PROBLEM

The issue of supranational organizations suggests the broader theme of legal transplants and their role in tax policy. That many substantive laws move from one country to another is a basic proposition of comparative law.[17] But institutional structures are often transplanted as well, so that a particular country's tax or other institutions often reflect another country's history as much or more than its own. We have already observed an extreme case of this in in Israel, India, and other postcolonial countries, whose entire tax systems were originally conceived in other places. A less extreme case involves the import of compliance mechanisms and sometimes entire taxes from the United States and other "advanced" countries to other developed (and some less developed) nations.

It is sometimes assumed that institutions and other formal arrangements are easy to change while underlying substantive rules are more resilient. In fact, the opposite is often true: institutions can stick around even when the underlying beliefs and

[17] The classic work is Alan Watson, *Legal Transplants: An Approach to Comparative Law* (Athens: University of Georgia Press, 1993). Tax transplants are discussed further in Chapter 6.

values that produced them have long disappeared. (The Electoral College, and even the United States Senate, are sometimes cited as examples.) A country may thus find that its tax structure not only resembles that of another country, but one which the original owner has long since discarded. (The issue of tax transplants is discussed further in Chapter 6.)

## 3.9 SUMMARY: TOWARD A COMPREHENSIVE MODEL OF TAX CULTURE

With Chapters 1 and 2 behind us, we can begin to describe something approaching a comprehensive model of tax culture, which may then be applied to specific issues and countries. This definition would involve both attitudes toward tax issues and the institutions which convert those attitudes into policy, or (in some cases) shape the attitudes themselves. For the sake of convenience, we have described the study of tax attitudes as "tax anthropology" and of tax institutions as "tax sociology," although this is in a sense a misnomer: both disciplines can be applied to either subject, the difference being one of emphasis rather than essence.

Tax attitudes would include issues like compliance or noncompliance, the individual or collective orientation of the society in question, and the respect or lack of respect for political and economic elites in the society. These attitudes might be consistent throughout a society, or might vary between regions, ethnicities, or socioeconomic groups, and with respect to different types of tax issues: indeed, this consistency or inconsistency would itself be an important factor in shaping its tax culture. Both the attitudes of the average taxpayer and those of the "tax elite" – lawyers, economists, accountants, government officials, and so forth – would be of interest here.

Tax institutions would include the full range of decision-making bodies, including legislative, administrative, and judicial bodies, as well as private sector organizations like law and accounting firms, educational institutions, that condition tax outcomes. International organizations and transplanted or borrowed norms may also play an important role, particularly in younger and smaller nations. Both tax attitudes and institutions would be supplemented by historical contingency or circumstance, so that a country or a region's tax culture may reflect events in an earlier period rather than structures or opinions that its people would choose today. In some cases, these quirks or contingencies might be of secondary importance, while in others they would predominate.

While tax culture employs broad generalities, it is best and perhaps only observed in specifics, by means of detailed, "thick" description of a given society or societies at a given time. This is the lesson both of cultural anthropologists (e.g., Geertz) and of tax scholars (e.g., Steinmo), whose best work tends to be focused on one or a relatively small number of societies. Collaborative studies between lawyers and professional social scientists (anthropologists, sociologist, political scientists) appear to have a special potential in this field, bridging the gap between theory and practice and allowing for a depth of analysis otherwise impossible.

## 3.10 TAX CULTURE IN ACTION: THE UNITED STATES AND SCANDINAVIA

With the above in mind, and before moving to later chapters, it may be useful to provide a relatively brief example of tax culture in action. This is done more comprehensively below, but I can already hear skeptics asking, like the contrary child at the idealized Passover Seder, "what is the point of all this and where exactly is it leading?"[18] Lawyers in particular are wont to demand a practical application for any theoretical exercise.

To get an idea of tax culture, consider a simple question: why is tax policy so different in the United States and the Scandinavian or Nordic countries (Sweden, Norway, Denmark, and Finland).[19] Anyone who has studied the matter knows, or thinks they know, that Scandinavians pay higher taxes than Americans and seem to do so willingly. (This is actually true of individual taxes, although rather less so for corporate and other business levies.) By contrast, Americans have a strong antitax tradition, resisting new taxes and (sometimes) rebelling against the payment of old ones. Indeed, conservatives sometimes cite Scandinavia as the kind of place Americans wouldn't want to live in. Why is this true, and how (for those who care to) might this situation be changed?

If you pose this question to most people, they would probably say: because Scandinavians are more liberal/collectivist than Americans and have a different trade-off between taxes and spending, especially for welfare benefits. Some might trace these differences back to the Viking tradition, the cold weather in Scandinavia, or the personality of Olof Palme and other recent Scandinavian leaders. On the other side, they might cite the Stamp Tax, the Whiskey Rebellion, or other examples of American's supposedly antitax heritage. More sophisticated observers might note that Scandinavian taxes are not really quite so high as they seem, that taxes net of reciprocal benefits are still lower, and so forth.[20] Depending on the politics of the individual in question, they might see the Scandinavian model as good or bad, but

18 The four sons (children) are historically categorized as wise, contrary, simple, and a fourth child who is not even capable of formulating a question. "Contrary" is sometimes rendered as "wicked."

19 I have been told by residents that "Scandinavia" is an incorrect term and one should always say "Nordic countries" or simply "Norden," which translates roughly as "The Northland." I am further told that one should properly include Iceland, the Faroe Islands, and perhaps (historically speaking) Estonia in the geographic mix. For tax purposes, it seems best to limit it to the nations listed.

20 See generally Henrik Jacobsen Kleven, "How Can Scandinavians Tax So Much?" www.henrikkleven.com/uploads/3/7/3/1/37310663/kleven_jep_july2014.pdf. Kleven offers a variety of possible answers to his own question, including both technical aspects of Nordic tax design and administration and underlying cultural differences, although conceding that the latter are difficult to transfer between nations.

most likely they would trace it back to some combination of the factors indicated above.[21]

A cultural analysis would not gainsay any of these conclusions (except perhaps the Viking one), but it would provide a more comprehensive framework for approaching the question. For example, in addition to examining taxpayer attitudes, one would have to study tax and other institutions in the countries in question. One would learn, for instance, that a rather large part of tax revenues in the Nordic countries stays close to home – they have small populations and part of tax revenue usually stays in one's own region – and that the national tax agencies have invested substantial resources in developing a "service" rather than "enforcement" orientation, at least for public relations purposes.[22] One might also learn that the Nordic countries are actually rather different in their taxation and fiscal policies, and that the notion of a single, unified "Nordic Model" is to some degree a function of outside marketing rather than any inherent reality.[23]

Turning to history, one would learn that the concept of the "welfare state" is actually a quite recent one in these countries, dating to the 1930s and sometimes more recently, and resulted from specific political trade-offs rather than deep-seated attitudinal differences. (Much of the nucleus for the Swedish welfare state was hammered out at a resort near Stockholm in 1938.) Geographical quirks, such as the proximity of the Nordic countries to the former Soviet Union and (earlier on) Nazi Germany would also play a role, the welfare state having originally been conceived as an alternative to these totalitarian models as well as to a more open, Anglo-Saxon style capitalism. Indeed, many of the ideas contributing to the Nordic Model were actually developed outside the region.[24] None of these developments were inevitable, but were the products of specific actions and decisions that could easily have gone in a different direction.

Moving beyond taxes, one might note that other aspects of Nordic society – gender equity, residential patterns, and perhaps even resistance to new immigrants (who people fear will demand welfare benefits before paying the offsetting taxes) – are closely tied to the country's tax and welfare systems, so that it is very difficult to change one part of the system without changing the others.[25] One might also note

[21] I develop these arguments further in a forthcoming book, *Dreamworld or Dystopia: The Nordic Modeland Its Influence in the Twenty-First Century* (Cambridge University Press) (anticipated publication 2021).

[22] See Chapter 2.

[23] See M. Livingston, *Dreamworld or Dystopia*, Chapter 3.

[24] See Sheri Berman, *The Primacy of Politics: Social Democracy and the Making of Europe's Twentieth Century* (Cambridge University Press, 2006).

[25] For a good and relatively recent study of the Nordic Model in economics, society, and culture see Mary Hilson, *The Nordic Model: Scandinavia Since 1945* (2008). For a more colloquial argument see Anu Partanen, *The Nordic Way in Everything: In Search of a Better Life* (2016). Partanen, who moved from Finland to the United States for personal reasons, also asserts that she spent a good deal more time on her American than her Finnish taxes. For a lighter, arguably tongue-in-cheek puncturing of the so-called Nordic Myth, see Michael Booth, *The Almost Nearly Perfect People: Beyond the Myth of the Scandinavian Utopia* (London: Picador Press, 2016).

the degree to which certain behavior patterns, including high labor force participation and the prevalence of part-time work, were responses to public policy rather than an impetus for them: for example, there is substantial evidence that gender equity in Sweden arose as a means of increasing tax revenues, rather than a particular Nordic tradition of equality or fairness.

Nordic tax culture would, in other words, be revealed to be part of a broader series of economic, political, and social arrangements rather than a freestanding actor: a subculture, if you will, rather than a separate, independent system. In evaluating this subculture, institutions would likely play as great or greater a role than popular attitudes, and historical quirks or contingencies would arguably play the most significant role of all. This is before one even reached more microscopic issues like the differences between the various Nordic countries or regions within each of them. An analysis of the American side would similarly examine attitudes, institutions, and historical or geographic contingencies rather than trying to draw a straight line from popular preferences to tax results. For example, the federalism and the (rather unusual) method of tax legislation in the United States, together with the size of the country and its (still important) regional differences, might play a larger role in shaping American tax policy than the Revolutionary War or the supposed tradition of tax resistance. Historical contingencies, like Norway having long been controlled by Denmark and Finland by Sweden, would play an equal or greater role on the Nordic side.

Finally – and no less important – one has to take into account the degree to which any country's or region's presentation of its tax culture may be a product of self-promotion or even self-deception as well as factual reality. The Nordic tax world was recently shaken by allegations that the Danish tax administration – one of the most admired in the world – was defrauded of hundreds of millions of kronor by a single taxpayer, very possibly with the assistance of a corrupt agency employee.[26] An earlier series of stories found that a number of Nordic politicians, some of whom had publicly lauded the concept of tax fairness, had themselves invested in a series of highly questionable overseas tax shelters. This does not mean that the Nordic tax systems are not unusually efficient, or that the regional commitment to tax fairness is somehow bogus or insincere. But it does suggest that they be balanced with a small dose of skepticism.

Tax culture is not rocket science, nor does it detract from the detailed description of tax realities (tax rates, exemptions, compliance mechanisms, etc.) that forms part of a more conventional analysis. But it does suggest a framework that permits one to strike a balance between ignoring noneconomic factors altogether, on the one hand, and consigning them to the realm of inexplicable and unapproachable cultural differences, on the other. That something is not easy to quantify does not necessarily mean that it is not subject to description, or cannot be part of a proper academic analysis. You just have to dig a little bit deeper.

[26] See David Segal, "Where in the World Is Denmark's $2 Billion?", *N. Y. Times*, October 5, 2018, www.nytimes.com/2018/10/05/business/denmark-skat-tax-scandal.html.

# 4

# Convergence, Divergence, and the Persistence of National Differences

The globalization phenomenon and its attendant limitations are by now so well-known as to require no introduction. In the happy version of the story, nations converge around a consensus of political democracy, open markets, and the "end of history" as we once knew it.[1] In the less happy version the phenomenon is a thinly veiled rationale for racism, oppression, and the resurgence of an American-dominated empire.[2] The truth is somewhere in between: one way or another, the concept is here to stay.

In theory, taxation should be a prime candidate for globalization. The internationalization of capital flows means that investors will tend to seek lower or at very least comprehensible tax rates, and countries that fail to provide this solution will suffer the consequences. The complex nature of taxation places a premium on technical expertise that at least in theory crosses national boundaries. Moreover, tax, or at all events income tax, is a relatively new area of law with few of the ties to religious or other natural law concepts that might affect (say) criminal, property, or family law. Money is money everywhere; and, with apologies to Oliver Wendell Holmes, there is probably no one in the real world who prefers higher to lower taxes. Based on these factors, we might be justified in expecting a higher degree of convergence in tax than in other areas of law.

Against this rosy view must be raised a number of red flags. First, the technical nature of tax is to some degree misleading. While some tax issues are undoubtedly technical in nature – think of the foreign tax credit rules or the consolidated return regulations – the underlying structure of tax systems is highly political and implicates deeply held values. In discussing tax progressivity or the allocation of tax burdens, technical expertise may be useless or regarded with a high degree of public skepticism. Both the French and American Revolutions broke out in part over tax issues, although it is possible that better policy could have averted them.

[1] See Francis Fukuyama, *The End of History and the Last Man* (New York: Free Press, 1992).

[2] See Michael Hardt & Antonio Negri, *Empire* (Cambridge: Harvard University Press, 2000); Amy Chua, *World on Fire: How Exporting Free Market Democracy Breeds Ethnic Hatred and Global Instability* (New York: Doubleday, 2002).

Second, and related, the appeal to universal values is itself politically tainted. While free trade and Western-style democracy may seem like neutral principles to many Americans, they are less likely to be regarded that way in China, India, and many developing countries. The tax policies that attend these values may be similarly controversial in other countries. This is an obvious point, but it is one that bears repeating, and is easily forgotten in the echo chamber of contemporary tax debates.

Finally – even if tax were a purely technical field and all actors shared the same basic values – there would remain the attitudinal and institutional differences described in Chapters 2 and 3, that is, the underlying problem of tax culture. The differences described in these chapters mean that, even when countries adopt the same superficial tax rules, they will be interpreted differently and come to have different meanings in different societies. To these differences must be added the self-interest of national governments that will tend to defend their prerogatives and resist ceding authority to international bodies. This is particularly true in a world in which many other forms of sovereignty, notably tariffs and other trade barriers, have already been ceded and tax policy remains one of the few areas governed almost exclusively at the national level.

This chapter considers the issue of globalization and convergence in taxation against the backdrop of tax culture, as developed in the preceding chapters. After a brief theoretical introduction, the chapter turns to two specific developments: the experience of supranational organizations, notably the EU and the OECD, and the role of educational programs – notably US-based LL.M. and other graduate programs – as described in the preceding chapter. While these organizations have helped to promote a "global tax culture," especially in developed countries, they are also subject to serious limitations that cast doubt on the development of such a culture.

Although emphasizing primary evidence, this chapter also considers the work of previous scholars who have studied the convergence problem. In particular the work of Alison Christians on international tax organizations, Assaf Likhovski on tax transplants, and Ruth Mason on EU tax problems will receive considerable attention. While each of these scholars has noted a tendency toward convergence in tax matters, each has also noted the limitations of that phenomenon, in ways that are broadly consistent with the themes developed herein.

## 4.1 BACKGROUND: GLOBALIZATION AS AN ECONOMIC, CULTURAL, AND LEGAL PHENOMENON

Globalization has been defined as "the development of an increasingly integrated global economy marked especially by free trade, free flow of capital, and the tapping of cheaper foreign labor markets."[3] A somewhat more systematic definition, taken from a major financial newspaper, refers to "a process by which national and regional economies, societies, and cultures have become integrated through the global network of trade, communication, immigration and transportation," adding that while it originally emphasized economics, "more recently the term has been expanded to include a broader range of areas and activities such as culture, media, technology, socio-cultural, political, and even biological factors, e.g. climate change." But the latter definition also sounds a cautionary note, explaining that "after the fall of the Berlin Wall, some talked about the rise of a 'one world way' of doing business and living, but more recent events have suggested that those thoughts were misplaced as we see the success of a number of varying economic and national systems."[4] Other definitions are broadly similar, albeit with differing emphases depending on the perspective of the observer.[5]

As might be expected, globalization has attracted a broad range of enthusiasts and critics, ranging from "one worlders" who predict the disappearance of national economies and cultures to those who see the entire concept as a rationalization for economic inequality and injustice. A recent sociology textbook divides observers into three different camps, which it rather colorfully labels the Skeptics, the Transformationalists, and the Hyperglobalizers.[6] The Hyperglobalizers argue that globalization is a sort of juggernaut that will ultimately sweep everything from its path, producing long-term benefits albeit with some inevitable short-term costs. Thomas Friedman of the New York Times is, or at least was, an apostle of this camp. The Skeptics believe that the current level of interdependence is merely a more intense version of a phenomenon that has existed since at least the nineteenth century, and that national governments remain important in setting agendas and coordinating economic activity. Regionalism, rather than globalism, appears to them the most likely outcome.

The Transformationalists occupy a middle position, seeing globalization as the common theme among diverse economic, political, and social developments, but with many of the old patterns in economics and society remaining. The Transformationalists tend to emphasize culture as well as economics and to see globalization as a two-way flow of ideas and influences rather than a process emanating from one central location. This also suggests that the globalization process may to some degree be reversible by local or regional action. (The author of this book is

3 Merriam-Webster Online Dictionary (June 24, 2015), www.merriam-webster.com/dictionary/globalization.

4 Financial Times/ft.com lexicon (June 24, 2015), http://lexicon.ft.com/Term?term=globalisation.

5 A Google search for "Globalization Definition" produced several million hits, although this is admittedly a less than scientific measure. Addition of the preferred British spelling ("globalisation") produces even more.

6 A. Giddens, M. Duneier, R. Appelbaum, & D. Carr, *Introduction to Sociology* (7th ed.) (New York: W.W. Norton & Co., 2009). The authors of the book appear to be located primarily in the Transformationalist camp.

somewhere between a Skeptic and a Transformationalist, although he has also learned to be skeptical of his own views, so that he is perhaps more accurately described as confused.)

Perhaps because of their anchoring in national law, legal scholars have often been reluctant to use the term globalization, and legal theory has often lagged behind economics, sociology, and other social sciences in this area. Writing in 2013, Ralf Michaels divides globalization into three aspects – reality, theory, and ideology – which are distinct from one another but interact in various ways.[7] Underlying all three areas is a change in the fundamental nature of the state, which has historically been understood to include three elements – territory, citizenship, and government – all three of which have been transformed beyond recognition by economic and political changes. Building upon the previous work of Philip Jessup, Michaels concludes by trying to develop a new theory, which he calls transnational law, which encompasses these diverse elements while avoiding some of the extremes of more traditional globalization theory.

Globalization is sometimes confused with the Americanization of law, as if comparative law consisted of nothing more than teaching foreigners American rules, institutions, and values. Ugo Mattei has argued that this is one reason for the continuing dearth of comparativists in American law schools: why study foreign law when it has nothing of value to teach us? Mattei notes, for example, that most international LL.M. programs involve teaching foreigners American law rather than engaging in a truly mutual exchange process.[8] (This is especially true of international tax programs.) Yet things may not be quite as depressing as Mattei suggests. International contacts inevitably have an effect on both parties, and as America becomes less dominant in the world economy, the process is likely to become more and more balanced.[9]

On a related note, Michael Barr and Reuven Avi-Yonah note that the globalization of law is often linked to the concept of economic development, the argument being that more advanced and universal legal rules will help developing countries to attract investment and achieve prosperity.[10] The authors suggest that, while there is some substance to this theory, its veracity depends upon what rules are adopted and

7 Ralf Michaels, "Globalization and Law: Law Beyond the State," in Banakar & Travers (eds.), *Law And Social Theory* (Oxford: Hart Publishing, 2013).

8 See Ugo Mattei, "An Opportunity Not to Be Missed: The Future of Comparative Law in the United States," *American Journal of Comparative Law*, 56 (1998), 709.

9 See also Martin Shapiro, "The Globalization of Law," *Indiana Journal of Legal Studies*, 1 (1993), 37, 37–38 ("when we speak of the globalization of law, we must be conscious that we are speaking of an extremely narrow, limited, and specialized set of legal phenomena ... We will almost always discover that we are really talking about North America, Europe, Australia, and New Zealand ... Indeed, much of the time, the globe will turn out to be the U.S. and Western Europe with shadowy addenda.")

10 See Michael S. Barr & Reuven S. Avi-Yonah, "Globalization, Law and Development: Introduction and Overview," *Michigan Journal of International Law*, 26 (2004), 1. The paper was a summary and overview of presentations at a conference on Globalization, Law, and Development held at the Michigan Law School.

whether they are connected to policies that encourage both economic development and a fair allocation of resources. Barr and Avi-Yonah further note that this is not the first period characterized by increased interconnectedness between nations, and that the most notable previous example of such a period – that between roughly 1870 and 1914 – collapsed amidst war, trade barriers, and other unpleasant developments.

If one focuses on tax law, the situation is something of a mixed bag. As noted above, tax law is relatively recent in origin, so that old distinctions like civil versus common law become less important. The technical nature of tax – its supposed basis in "universal" economic concepts – likewise favors a high degree of convergence, as does the mobility of capital, which will in theory seek the best (or at least the lowest) available taxes. But there are countervailing factors, notably the historic connection of taxing authority and national sovereignty, to a degree greater than most areas of law. Even when tax rates are similar, income is often defined in a different way, and variations in enforcement mean that taxes paid may differ even when the laws on paper are the same. These factors militate against a rapid convergence of taxes and suggest that, when it does occur, convergence may be superficial in nature, producing tax systems that are similar on the surface but diverge in the details.

The result is that tax shows a significant tendency toward convergence, but one that depends a great deal on what country and what provision is in question. As a general rule, business taxes show the strongest pattern of convergence, individual taxes tend to be more resistant, and the details of tax administration and enforcement – what actually happens as opposed to what happens on paper – are most resistant of all.[11] Different countries also respond differently to external pressures: European countries are perhaps the most subject to convergence, while China, with an economy larger than many geographic regions, regularly defies conventional norms and suffers few consequences for doing so.[12] This follows the pattern in other areas of law, where fields of law that are associated with international capital flows (e.g., corporate, antitrust, or copyright law) demonstrate a relatively high degree of convergence, while those more associated with local norms and values (e.g., criminal and family law) remain more different, and countries that are strong enough to resist international pressure are often significant outliers even in the earlier fields.

The patterns above are not surprising, nor are they especially new: comparativists in Europe and elsewhere have long noted that certain provisions converge more rapidly than others or (what amounts to the same thing) that the "presumption of similarity" is more applicable for certain types of law, and for certain countries, than it is for others. That comparative law has traditionally emphasized a small number of European nations – the United Kingdom, France, Germany, occasionally Italy, and later the United States – tends at times to submerge this problem but never

[11] See Chapter 6 (discussing convergence and nonconvergence of various substantive rules).
[12] See Chapter 5 (discussing the tax culture of China, India, and other nations).

completely eliminates it.[13] While possessed of certain unique features, tax law is broadly consistent with this overall pattern.

Tax law is frequently compared to trade law, because both involve international capital flows, and because the trade analogy is frequently applied in tax cases. A fundamental difference is that there is no international agreement to standardize tax practices and no single group like the World Trade Organization (WTO) to ensure compliance with its terms. Thus, when tax laws converge, it is by means of voluntary agreements or the medium of persuasion, where one country – whether because it is genuinely convinced that its rules and practices need changing or fears that it will lose business and investment if it doesn't change them – adopts rules and practices similar to those of another country. Even when countries participate in regional organizations, like the EU, they do so on a voluntary basis, and the authority of the organization varies enormously depending on the kinds of taxes involved. While there is undoubtedly a measure of compulsion in these agreements, the process remains conceptually distinct.

An understanding of "tax globalization" accordingly requires us to consider the processes by which voluntary agreement takes place, and what factors retard as well as encourage this process. For convenience's sake, I have divided these processes into three categories: formal convergence, by means of international organizations; informal convergence, by means of educational and other information-sharing programs; and convergence by example, in which one country adopts another country's rule or practice simply because it believes it to be better than its existing rule (the so-called tax transplant phenomenon). The first two of these themes are dealt with mostly in this chapter, while the third is introduced here and developed further in Chapter 6.

## 4.2 FORMAL CONVERGENCE: THE ROLE OF INTERNATIONAL ORGANIZATIONS

### 4.2.1 *European Union (EU)*

When people talk about the role of international organizations in tax policy, they typically begin with the European Union. There is a certain logic to this: Brexit notwithstanding, the EU has been a remarkably successful organization, and its power in tax and other matters exceeds that of any other regional entity. Yet the EU's influence in tax matters turns out to be surprisingly tenuous, conceptually

13 A recent edition of the classic Schlesinger text on comparative law suggests some change in this area: the book both includes extensive examples of Asian, African, and Latin American law and takes a "topical" approach to comparative law, suggesting that convergence may be more extensive in some subjects or regions than others. The book's discussion of cultural and ideological issues, and the related tendency of Americans to confuse comparative law with the imposition of Anglo-American norms, is also quite welcome. Ugo A. Mattei, Teemu Ruskola, & Antonio Gidi, *Schlesinger's Comparative Law* (7th ed.) (New York: Foundation Press, 2009).

dependent on the relationship between tax and trade policy and politically limited by the reluctance of Member States to surrender sovereignty in tax matters.

The EU developed in stages, beginning with the European Coal and Steel Community (1951), proceeding to the European Economic Community (EEC or Common Market) in 1957, and becoming the European Union only in 1993. As the group has expanded in function, it has likewise expanded in size, from six to the current twenty-eight members. The simultaneous expansion of size and function has created predictable strains, and the impending departure of the United Kingdom has forced a reconsideration of goals and methods even by the original core members, some of whose concerns are not entirely different from those of the UK.

The EU began as a tariff union, and its tax jurisdiction flows largely from its trade powers. The problem is an obvious one. Let us imagine that France eliminates tariffs on German imports but imposes a 20-percent value added tax, which is imposed on imports but rebated on export items.[14] Assume further that there is no equivalent German tax. Plainly this has the effect of a tariff and violates the principle of free trade in spirit if not in letter. This situation would be prohibited by EU law, which requires that VAT be imposed within a narrow "band" of acceptable rates (historically between 15 and 20 percent) and that they be effectively neutral as between goods domestically produced and imported goods.

Income taxes are more complicated. Suppose that France and Germany each have a 30-percent income tax, but France, wishing to encourage domestic manufacturing, reduces its rate to 20 or 10 or even zero percent. Since there is no obligation to maintain a particular rate structure under EU law – and since the reduction would not facially discriminate between French-produced or German-produced goods – this provision would not of itself violate EU norms. But supposing that France wants to help a particular region – say, the southern or southwestern part of the country – and makes the reduced rate applicable only in that geographic area? Or suppose that the reduction applies only to a particular industry (cars, wine, heavy industry) that is suffering from German competition and which the French government wants to help out? Or suppose that the rules are written in such a way that, in substance if not form, they exempt or significantly favor French over German or other foreign concerns? At some point the targeted tax reduction will begin to look a lot like a trade subsidy and undermine the essential purpose of a tariff-free zone. If there are enough of these provisions, and they are enacted by enough countries, the entire system will be in danger of collapse.

To draw this line, the EU has developed a complex jurisprudence, which is difficult to describe but remains inevitable if the principle of national tax sovereignty is to be reconciled with the principle of free trade. (The US commerce clause comes inevitably to mind). The essence is that tax differences are not inherently unacceptable, but become so when they have an effect of discrimination in favor of domestic

14 Rebates on exports are in fact fairly typical of VATs.

goods or services (i.e., trade subsidies) or against their foreign equivalents. Of course, the entire problem could be avoided if the Member States would harmonize their income as well as their VAT tax rates, and this solution has indeed been proposed by many observers, especially in the larger states (read France and Germany) that are afraid of losing business to lower-tax jurisdictions. But it has proved politically infeasible, and in the current environment appears to be more or less on hold.

In a 2007 article, American tax scholar Ruth Mason considers EU tax jurisprudence and its differences from the American model.[15] Mason notes that the United States and the EU are forced to consider many similar problems, including tax discrimination by Member States; double taxation and harmonization of tax bases; and the questions of incentives, subsidies, and interstate competition. But the difference in political structures means these problems will be confronted in a very different matter. In particular, the balance in tax lawmaking authority – tilted toward the federal government in the United States but remaining almost wholly at the state level in the EU – means that it will be difficult to achieve the level of standardization in Europe, especially for income taxes, that Americans are familiar with, as well as being much more difficult to articulate common positions in negotiations with outsiders. Notwithstanding these differences, Mason believes that the United States and the EU can learn from each other with respect to common problems, particularly in the harmonization of tax systems across regional and cultural lines.

One practical problem with tax harmonization – in the EU or elsewhere – is that different countries define income in different ways. Let us assume that France, Germany, Italy, and the remaining EU countries agree on a common individual, corporate, and estate tax rate. The agreement may mean little if the countries maintain different rules for computing income, deductions, and credits, so that the same factual situation will produce different amounts of taxable income. Even an identical tax code may produce different results if administration, enforcement, and taxpayer behavior diverge in different countries.[16] Presumably it would be possible to harmonize these practices as well, but that is a long and difficult process, and perhaps accounts for some of the reluctance to tackle the harmonization issue more directly.

The EU thus provides an interesting example of tax cooperation but also of its limitations. European countries share a millennium-old tradition and the project of European unity has been going forward, with fits and starts, for more than sixty years. If these countries are unable to agree on common tax principles, how likely is convergence of tax policy among countries on different continents and with different political, social, and legal systems? Is the convergence between such countries

[15] Ruth Mason, "Common Markets, Common Tax Problems," *Florida Law Review*, 8 (2007), 599. Mason's article was written in a period of relative optimism regarding the future of the EU, before Brexit and similar movements that have questioned the European integration project.

[16] This "same words, different meaning" phenomenon is addressed further in Chapter 5.

likely to be profound or more superficial in nature, providing nominally similar rules but with significant and persistent differences in actual practice? The difference between tax and trade policy is particularly striking here. How and why is it that European nations share a "common market" in trade but demonstrate only limited coordination in tax matters, with such coordination as there is depending largely on the trade analogy? Does this result from the peculiar history of European integration, or would similar problems exist elsewhere?

### 4.2.2 *IMF, OECD, and Other "Global" Organizations*

Outside of Europe, regional organizations tend to have somewhat less influence on tax policy. NAFTA, ASEAN, Mercosur, and so forth are essentially trade organizations that get involved in tax issues only as a byproduct of their other activities. The World Trade Organization (WTO), formerly the General Agreement on Tariffs and Trade (GATT), is likewise primarily a trade organization and has relatively little influence on tax policy.[17] Because taxes can at times function as trade barriers, these organizations are not wholly irrelevant to tax policy, but there role is usually secondary in this area. International cooperation in other specialized matters (antitrust, copyright, etc.) likewise does not usually extend to tax matters.

The role of international organizations is somewhat greater in developing countries. Although nominally free to pursue their own policies, developing countries frequently face strong pressure to conform to international norms and expectations – or, more bluntly, the norms and expectations of the people and organizations, especially banks and other financial institutions, that they depend upon economically. Sometimes this pressure is indirect, but at times it is more immediate, and not always especially subtle.

The International Monetary Fund (IMF), an organization of lender nations, has come under particular criticism for pressuring debtor nations to adopt fiscal and monetary policies that reflect the interests of their creditors and local elites and may harm the remaining citizens of the countries in question. These policies typically emphasize spending cuts and free market economic reforms, but sometimes include reductions in taxes or more regressive tax policy as well. Some of the criticism of the IMF has come from human rights and similar activists, but some of it has come from mainstream economists. Joseph Stiglitz, who served as the World Bank's chief economist for three years, has written eloquently and on occasion somewhat caustically about this problem.[18]

17 Why precisely the nations of the world got together on trade rather than tax policy is an interesting question. Part of the answer appears to be that trade barriers were perceived, rightly or wrongly, as among the causes of previous conflicts (notably World War II) in a way that does not really apply to taxation. See Douglas A. Irwin, *Against the Tide: An Intellectual History of Free Trade* (Princeton University Press, 1996).

18 Joseph E. Stiglitz, *Globalization and Its Discontents* (New York: W.W. Norton & Co., 2002). Similar issues are addressed in Amy Chua, *op. cit.* 2.

There are also a number of organizations that attempt to coordinate the tax policies of the developed countries, although typically on the basis of persuasion rather than compulsion. Prominent among these is the Organization for Economic Cooperation and Development (OECD), which is essentially a club of the wealthier and more powerful nations, and which sponsors numerous conferences and studies on fiscal matters as well as gathering statistics and other information on the subject. The International Bureau of Fiscal Documentation (IBFD) in Amsterdam likewise provides a clearinghouse for tax information, although it appears to be more geared toward private users attempting to reduce their own tax burdens rather than broader public policy concerns.

The OECD is an especially interesting case. Being composed of wealthy, powerful nations it must operate primarily on a consensus basis. Yet its influence remains considerable. This is particularly true for international tax rules, in which it may be the only significant player other than the individual nations themselves. The ability to claim neutrality or impartiality, at least where the richer nations are concerned, may be a significant advantage in this process. The sheer volume of statistics and other data gathered by the OECD – now largely computerized and frequently available only through the organization and its subsidiaries – provides it with still further influence.

The website of the OECD Center for Tax Policy and Administration (CTP) suggests the range and depth of its tax interests.[19] The website lists no fewer than a dozen different projects, ranging from Aggressive tax planning to Transfer pricing and including such additional subjects as Consumption tax, Tax treaties, Tax administration, and so forth. The website also includes a link to the OECD Tax Database, which includes a veritable cornucopia of current and historical tax statistics, ranging from personal and corporate income taxes to consumption and value added taxes, tax burdens on wage income, and various other subjects. The database provides still further links to a bevy of publications, conveniently available in both hard copy and electronic versions, on these and other subjects. A publication entitled Revenue Statistics: 1965–2016, available in both English and French, is a special highlight, going on for some 340 pages (all free of charge) and rivaling the World Almanac for the range and depth of its statistical coverage.[20] These links are primarily informational in nature, but as the old saying goes, knowledge is power: in the absence of other sources of information they have an inevitable influence on how individual countries understand tax issues and what policy choices they make in response.

The Base Erosion and Profit-Shifting study, known popularly as BEPS, is a particular example of the OECD's tax influence. The organization's website defines BEPS to include "tax avoidance strategies that exploit gaps and mismatches

19 www.oecd.org/ctp/.

20 https://read.oecd-ilibrary.org/taxation/revenue-statistics-1965–2016_9789264283183-en#page1.

in tax rules to artificially shift profits to low- or no-tax jurisdictions."[21] This innocuous-sounding phrase is broad enough to address virtually any subject in international tax law. Thus, the BEPS project has at various times addressed the attribution of profits to a permanent establishment (BEPS Action 7); profit-shifting from developing country mining enterprises by means of excessive interest deductions (BEPS Action 4); tax challenges arising from digitalization; and numerous other issues. Nor is the project just talk: at least one international agreement (the Multilateral Convention to Implement Tax Treaty Measures to Prevent BEPS) has already come into force, and other agreements will likely be secured in the future. The project is so influential that the term "BEPS" has become common parlance for international tax avoidance strategies and responses to them, even when the OECD is not directly involved.

The OECD's influence has also been significant in the areas of transfer pricing and (as was suggested above) the definition of a permanent establishment for international tax purposes.[22] Here as elsewhere, the organization's influence results from a formidable combination of technical expertise, information flows, and institutional reputation. For example, the OECD's Transfer Pricing Country Profiles include information on transfer pricing policies in no fewer than fifty-four different jurisdictions, the great majority of which are available at the click of a mouse.[23] The profiles both describe each jurisdiction's policies and the extent to which the policies follow (or do not follow) the OECD's own Transfer Pricing Guidelines, which were first published in 2017 and continue for some 612 pages.[24] It is difficult to imagine where else this information could be gathered without paying a very substantial, possibly ongoing fee.

The OECD is especially important in areas where policy tends to be set by a few large, wealthy, and powerful nations. For example, in transfer pricing, the main available definitions are those of the United States or of the OECD. In the absence of the organization, the United States might be even more dominant in this field than it is today.

One difficulty in assessing the influence of international organizations is that they tend to reflect outside pressures rather than creating them. In this connection it is often emphasized that tax treaties are bilateral in nature, a factor which supposedly distinguishes tax from trade, environment, and other areas that stress multilateral accords. Yet to paraphrase George Orwell, some treaties are more bilateral than others. In practice, the larger countries, like the United States, tend to proceed from "model treaties" that include a fixed set of provisions which they seek, with varying

21 www.oecd.org/ctp/beps/.

22 Income from a foreign corporation is typically subject to tax in the host country only if it is part of a so-called permanent establishment, a term which can be defined in various ways.

23 www.oecd.org/tax/transfer-pricing/transfer-pricing-country-profiles.htm.

24 www.oecd.org/tax/transfer-pricing/oecd-transfer-pricing-guidelines-for-multinational-enterprises-and-tax-administrations-20769717.htm.

degrees of success, to impose upon other countries. Indeed, the recommendations of international organizations like the OECD frequently (although not always) reflect the interests of these same countries to a large degree. Put differently, the line between national and international tax law, or between bilateral and multilateral agreements, may be a fuzzy one in the tax area, with both bilateral and multilateral agreements typically reflecting the interests of those with more bargaining power.

A similar problem arises with respect to large multinational corporations. In theory, these are private actors who respond to tax law rather than creating it. The reality is, of course, quite different: sophisticated businesses inevitably seek the most advantageous tax treatment and national tax policies are frequently made in response to their behavior. It is surely no accident that within a few years of the US tax reform act of 1986, most industrial nations had reduced their maximum income rates to somewhere below 50 percent, or that many have adopted technical rules (transfer pricing, financial reporting requirements, etc.) similar to the US rules. While some of these changes reflect intellectual influence, many result from a fear of losing business to countries with lower or more flexible tax rates. Even China, whom no one would call small or insignificant in nature, faces pressure to conform its tax system to internationally accepted norms.

The influence of international organizations may thus be partially a question of definition. With the possible exception of the EU, the developed nations maintain a formal independence in tax – especially income tax – matters that goes beyond that in other policy areas. This situation is unlikely to change soon: given current political developments, like Brexit and the US–China trade war, it may actually be accelerating. But formal independence is only part of the overall tax story. Notwithstanding recent developments, there remain substantial constraints on national tax policies, and a comprehensive understanding of tax culture must take these into account.

A good example of the blurring of national and international tax policy is the so-called Foreign Account Tax Compliance Act (FATCA), which requires foreign financial institutions to report on the assets held by US citizens and (if they fail to do so) subjects them to a sort of penalty withholding provision. FATCA was nominally a matter of US law, but its practical effects were primarily overseas: I was barely aware of it when many of my foreign contacts began to ask questions about it.[25] As the United States loses, or perhaps squanders, its international preeminence it is possible this sort of dictation to other countries will become less common. But for now the line between voluntary and involuntary agreement, and that between unilateral and multilateral decisions, remains a blurry one in the tax area. (FATCA remains highly

[25] There is a touching assumption that American law professors are up-to-date on all technical provisions of US law, an assumption foreigners (not to mention spouses) are quickly disabused of. Perhaps my after-tax income would be higher if I were less honest on this point.

unpopular and there are ongoing efforts to repeal it both in Congress and elsewhere: the fate of these efforts is unclear at the time of writing.)[26]

## 4.3 INFORMAL CONVERGENCE: THE ROLE OF EDUCATIONAL EXCHANGES

Ask any comparative law scholar when legal systems will converge, and she will likely answer: when everyone attends the same law school. Everyone does not yet attend the same law school, or even the same graduate tax program. But a lot of the most important tax policy-makers do attend one of a very small number of programs, and its effect on their thinking – notwithstanding the large number of competing influences – is unmistakable. Like all education, this effect manifests itself not only in the answer to tax questions, but in the way those questions are framed in the first place and the language that is used to discuss them. As any lawyer will tell you, how a question is framed is half the story, and tax is no exception.

Most of the leading international tax programs are located in the United States, primarily although not exclusively on the East Coast. NYU and Harvard are especially prominent, with Columbia, Georgetown, and Michigan not far behind. The website for the NYU program describes the purpose of these enterprises:

> The globalization of trade and investment flows is having a profound effect on the practices and policies of international taxation. To meet the needs of lawyers in an interrelated world, law schools must move beyond traditional programs in international taxation which deal only with the tax regimes of their countries … tax advisers, tax professors, and government tax officials increasingly must operate in a context in which knowledge of unilateral rules is inadequate.[27]

Harvard makes a similar appeal, adding for good measure that its program was founded pursuant to a UN Resolution and "for more than 50 years … has provided the finest available graduate education in taxation to future fiscal leaders and tax experts from all over the world."[28]

With the rise of English as an international language, international tax programs are no longer limited to North America. Such programs have proliferated especially in northern Europe, at universities like Oxford (UK), Leiden (Netherlands), Vienna, and various other locations. For example, the international tax LL.M. at Vienna offers full-time and part-time options, both exclusively in English, with the goal of enabling students to "skillfully apply international tax law in professional corporate, consulting, and administrative environments." The website for the program includes testimonials from several students, none of whom appear to be of Austrian extraction, attesting to the program's academic quality and value as

26 The opposition is strong, or well-heeled, enough to support both a web page and a Twitter handle. www.repealfatca.com (May 3, 2018); @RepealFatca (Twitter) (May 3, 2018).

27 www.law.nyu.edu/tax/academicprograms/internationaltaxprogramforforeignstudents (July 17, 2015).

28 www.law.harvard.edu/programs/about/tax/international-tax-program.html (July 17, 2015).

a growth experience. To emphasize the worldly nature of the program, the home page includes a photograph of five suitably international students with their hands on an oversized globe, smiling broadly.[29]

Allowing for the inevitable local variations, most international tax programs are pretty much the same. All include courses on international and comparative taxes, tax policy, tax planning, and assorted domestic tax subjects. Most are taught by a mix of adjuncts and full-time faculty. The programs overlap with but are to a significant degree distinct from domestic LL.M. programs, which tend to emphasize local tax issues. This difference is exacerbated for the American programs, since many foreign students complete a J.S.D. or other doctoral program, while relatively few American lawyers continue beyond a master's degree.[30] At the American schools in particular, a substantial percentage of foreign students are subsidized by their home governments, enabling them to cope with hefty tuitions and (not coincidentally) making the programs highly lucrative for the host institutions. Some students stay in the host country and never go home at all.[31]

What impact do the international tax programs have? It seems unlikely that they force any government to undertake policies which lack political support. But – like any educational program – they are important in framing the underlying policy debate. In particular, they tend to diffuse a certain pro-market, efficiency-oriented viewpoint that is common in the United States but historically less so in other countries. The American notion of "tax reform" – lower rates in return for a broader tax base and supposedly better compliance – tends to take hold among the students and (eventually) their home countries.[32] Intellectual trends thus reinforce tax competition in pushing tax rates downward, with or without the promised base broadening.

The concept of tax policy expertise, of a subject too important to be left to ordinary people, is likewise promoted by these programs in much the same way that Davos or similar gatherings promote the idea of an international elite in other, nontax matters.[33] Some of this elitism, as well, stays with the students when they return to their home countries.

A particularly interesting dynamic applies to students from countries, including former Eastern Bloc and many nonwestern nations, with a socialist economic and political tradition. Marxism is a comprehensive worldview that explains just about

29 www.international-tax-program.at (2019).

30 NYU and Georgetown have large domestic LL.M. programs, whereas Harvard's graduate tax program is primarily international in nature.

31 A problem not limited to tax programs. When I was a Cornell undergraduate, the basketball courts were full of foreign students who appeared to be in no hurry to return home. A government professor told me that he had seen a carrel, at Harvard, of a student in his 23rd year of graduate school.

32 This phenomenon may be slightly less common at European programs.

33 Davos lost some of its appeal when a number of participants, perhaps shaken by the populist movements in their home countries, decided to stop attending. See Charles Riley, "Davos no-shows reflect the world in a state of crisis," www.cnn.com (January 21, 2019).

everything in terms of economics. Lapsed Marxists are thus uniquely susceptible to law and economics, a similarly determinist philosophy that is equally indifferent to real-world evidence. I once spoke with an Israeli scholar who seemed surprised that the previously egalitarian country had a high GINI coefficient, increased unemployment, and other ills associated with rapid economic growth. "I don't understand it," he said innocently, "we did everything the Americans told us to do."

As in all universities, the most important part of international tax programs takes place outside the classroom. Whatever they learn in their courses, students at NYU, Harvard, and similar law schools spend a substantial period in the company of other tax professionals and – no less important – away from their own countries. Inevitably this makes them think a little bit less like Brazilians, Chinese, and so forth and a little bit more like English-speaking tax professionals. The NYU website uses this as a selling point, noting that "Students in the International Taxation program come from countries around the world, and they perennially [sic] form a strong bond with each other . . . students develop relationships with both US and non-US lawyers that last the rest of their careers."[34] European programs make similar claims.[35]

Supplementing educational programs are a bevy of international tax conferences, some of them sponsored by universities and others by independent organizations. Among the latter the International Fiscal Association (IFA) stands out in particular. In existence since 1938 and with its headquarters located in the Netherlands, the IFA describes itself as "the only non-governmental and non-sectoral organization dealing with fiscal matters" and claims almost 13,000 members in 114 countries.[36] The IFA sponsors a large number of global and international conferences and publishes a range of documents, among which the so-called *Cahiers de droit fiscal international*, now published in English notwithstanding the French title, have particular pride of pace.[37] The IFA and similar organizations provide a platform for exchange of tax knowledge and practices and a sort of continuing education in the tax field: together with the international tax programs they constitute perhaps the most vivid example of an international tax culture now in existence.

## 4.4 TAX PRACTICE AND THE PHENOMENON OF CONVERGENCE BY EXAMPLE

When students ask why they should study comparative law, they are frequently told that it will help them to make their own legal system better. (The alternative answer, "because it offers unlimited opportunities for free travel," is considered a little bit too cynical.) Indeed, a traditional purpose of comparative law is to identify the "better" or "best" rule in a given area of law and hope that countries which have less optimal

34 www.law.nyu.edu/llmjsd/internationaltaxation (July 17, 2015).
35 See the discussion of the Vienna program earlier in this same section.
36 www.ifa.nl/organisation/what_is_ifa/pages/default.aspx.
37 The *Cahiers*, which the IFA modestly refers to as its "masterpiece," have been published since 1939.

rules will ultimately come to adopt them. The phenomenon of so-called legal transplants, as identified by Alan Watson and other scholars, is from this perspective central to the legal enterprise.[38]

Because money is fungible, and because international capital transfers are relatively easy to accomplish, tax is a prime candidate for legal transplants. A couple who does not like American family law is unlikely to get married in Japan, although this does happen. By contrast, a company that believes American taxes are unfair, or simply too high, is quite likely to structure itself or its transactions to reduce its exposure to American taxes. At the extreme, businesses and individuals may physically move from one jurisdiction to another to reduce their taxes, although it is in most cases unnecessary to do so. There is thus greater pressure for countries to conform their tax systems to international norms than their criminal, family, or highway laws.

This economic pressure supplements, and is to some degree responsible for, the high degree of informational exchange in the tax field. In supervising student papers, I find that it is nearly always easier to find foreign tax law in English translation than other areas of legal practice, because more people – or in any event, more people with money – care about it, and it is accordingly more profitable to reproduce it.

How extensive is this convergence-by-example, or perhaps we should say convergence by the operation of market forces, in the tax field? It's a difficult question to answer, because there is no obvious way to quantify tax rules or measure their impact in different societies. Nevertheless, a few observations are in order.

First, the degree of convergence or transplanting depends a lot on the rule at stake. There is plainly a high degree of convergence in business tax rules, particularly in areas – think of installment sales or consolidated returns – that do not involve deeply held political or cultural values. The extent of borrowing is likely to be lower for rules that involve home offices, travel and entertainment expenditures, or other aspects of personal taxes and personal behavior. Even in the business area, it is striking how many basic principles remain different in different tax systems. It took decades for US tax authorities to accept the LLC (i.e., nonstock corporation) concept, which is nearly universal in Europe, and the level of "integration" between the American corporate and individual taxes remains lower than in many other countries. The treatment of charitable and other personal deductions demonstrates even less convergence. Even American states, which would in theory have similar values to the federal government, are distinctly resistant to convergence: New York's income tax plays off the federal system, but Pennsylvania retains a schedule approach which, I am told, has roots in British practice but almost nothing to do with that used by neighboring states. Several states have no income tax at all. (The question of which specific rules converge, or fail to converge, is considered in Chapter 6.)

[38] Legal transplants are discussed further in Chapter 6.

Second, rules on paper tend to converge much more readily than rules in practice. We mentioned earlier that, following the US tax reform of 1986, many other developed countries reduced their rates to something approaching the US levels. But these are nominal rates: they don't tell you much of anything about effective rates (i.e., after the impact of deductions, credits, etc. is considered) and nothing at all about the level of compliance, that is, the amount of tax collected in the real world and not merely on paper. Some wag once calculated that if all the taxes on the books in Italy were actually paid in full, they would amount to more than 100 percent of the country's GDP. This situation has perhaps improved in the interim, but it highlights the difficulty in measuring convergence by the laws on the books.

Finally – at the risk of some repetition – the difference in legal and economic cultures means that, even with the best of intentions, the same rule will have a different effect in different societies. A distinction between business and personal expenditures will have one meaning in a culture, like the United States, that traditionally draws a strict line between business and personal activities, and another in a Mediterranean or Middle Eastern culture that does not draw such a line. Depreciation tables will be of dubious efficacy in a country where people are not mathematically literate and do not have easy access to computers or similar technology.[39] Differential tax rates are more important in Europe, where countries are small and people frequently cross international borders, than they are in East Asia or North America. These differences become more significant as one moves away from the more elite business circles, which are likely to share agreed international norms, and into the mass of population that doesn't: recent elections in the United States, United Kingdom, and other countries provide a stark reminder of this difference. This "same rule, different meaning" phenomenon applies to convergence-by-example as much as the other forms.

Although it remains a young field, a number of previous scholars have considered the diffusion of tax rules and the various means – formal, informal, or somewhere in between – that they are spread. The work of Allison Christians, a Canadian–American scholar, is particularly impressive. In her article "Hard and Soft Law in International Taxation,"[40] Christians distinguishes between tax law as written in treaties and other international agreements (hard law) and that made in more informal arrangements between nations (soft law). According to the author, much of the sharing or spreading of tax provisions takes place within this second category. This makes the sharing or convergence more difficult to trace but no less significant in real-world practice. Christians cites the OECD's work on so-called harmful tax practices as a paradigmatic example of the soft law category, the OECD having no formal authority to impose tax law rules or concepts but its recommendations

39 I suspect that all businesspersons understand depreciation, but they may not all be that good at quantifying it.

40 *Wisconsin Journal of International Law*, 25 (2007), 325.

helping to shape the debate and carrying substantial weight with individual countries.[41] The OECD's work on transfer pricing and the efforts of the EU and IMF are cited as subsidiary examples.[42]

The work of other scholars, including Daniel Shaviro and Reuven Avi-Yonah, is also significant in this area. Avi-Yonah's book *International Tax as International Law* argues that international tax law is at bottom merely another form of international law, embodying shared principles like the source and residence rules or the avoidance of double taxation, which – while frequently honored in the breach – are no more or less coherent than those in other legal fields.[43] If Avi-Yonah's analysis is correct, one would expect that there would be significant convergence between countries, at least in provisions that affected cross-border transactions, and that divergence from these principles would be the exception rather than the rule. Daniel Shaviro's work, *Fixing U.S. International Taxation*, suggests a program for the reworking of US international tax rules, but with the suggestion that these might become a model for similar changes in the rules of other countries.[44] Scholarship of this type suggests a gradual transition from a world in which tax is a national concern subject to piecemeal international agreements to one in which it is a global concern subject to national variations: a bit more like the current trade regime and a bit less like the current tax reality. While neither Shaviro nor Avi-Yonah would suggest that we have arrived at that world yet, their work constitutes a small but significant step in that direction.

It must be remembered that the analyses above are generic in nature and may not consider the political and ideological differences that encourage resistance to convergence even when a new rule actually is "better" than an old one in an abstract sense. These differences are likely to be particularly potent in countries that have divergent political systems or different historical experiences, particularly when these experiences took place in the very recent past. In these latter cases history, ideology, or simply politics may prove more potent than generic policy arguments.

For example, Eastern European countries, with their recent experience of communism, have a radically different perspective on redistribution, by taxes or otherwise, than their Western neighbors.[45] China sees almost everything differently from the West and tends to resist conformity as a matter of national pride. India has a mix of European and non-European cultures that is difficult to fit into any pattern.[46] Put differently, there are pressures for convergence but offsetting and sometimes greater pressures in the opposite direction: policy outcomes reflect the interaction of these offsetting forces. This is no less true for tax than for other fields.

41 Ibid., 326–31.

42 Ibid., 332 n. 35.

43 Reuven S. Avi-Yonah, *International Tax as International Law: An Analysis of the International Tax Regime* (Cambridge University Press, 2007).

44 Daniel N. Shaviro, *Fixing U.S. International Taxation* (Oxford University Press, 2014).

45 See Chapter 6.

46 See Chapter 5.

## 4.5 AN ADDITIONAL NOTE ON TAX ARBITRAGE

It may be worth adding, at this point, an additional word on the tax arbitrage phenomenon.[47] Taxpayers, including multinational corporations and (to an increasing degree) wealthy individuals, tend to seek the most favorable tax treatment, and will frequently move money or resources to jurisdictions that provide it. This behavior is sometimes argued to be a powerful or even an irresistible force in favor of convergence between tax systems, since countries that fail to adjust their rules will lose business to those that do. How true is this in practice, and how important is it as compared to the other factors described above?

It isn't difficult to see the argument for tax arbitrage and why it is more important in tax than in other fields. Let's say that I am deciding to invest money in the United States or Switzerland, or that I have the option of starting a business in either country. If the marginal tax rate in the United States is 40 percent, and in Switzerland it is 20 percent, there is obviously some incentive for me to move in the Swiss rather than the American direction. The same is true if the nominal tax rates are 40 percent in both countries, but the Swiss tax system offers deductions, credits, and so forth that move the effective tax rate to the lower figure.

Assuming the existence of a perfect market, and assuming everything else in the two countries was the same, eventually so much money would move out of the United States that the US tax authorities would feel irresistible pressure to conform their tax practices to something more like the Swiss model. Nor does the difference have to be that dramatic: in theory, even a 1 or 2 percent difference in effective tax rates, like a small difference in interest rates, would be sufficient to compel the movement of vast quantities of money, until all countries felt the pressure to conform their tax rates to the optimal (and presumably the lowest) level. Indeed, everything else being equal, it would take only one country offering more generous tax benefits until all business and investment moved there and everyone else shut down.[48]

That said, the tax arbitrage argument – like the domestic "race to the bottom" in corporate and regulatory law – can easily be overstated. One obvious reason is the imperfection of markets and the difficulty of moving some (although not all) factors of production to countries with lower tax rates. But there are also several other considerations.

[47] Tax arbitrage has been defined as "the practice of profiting from differences between the way transactions are treated for tax purposes," typically involving the "restructur(ing of) transactions in the most advantageous way in order to pay the least amount of tax," www.investopedia.com/terms/t/tax-arbitrage.asp. Tax arbitrage may take place at a domestic or international level, but the opportunities are likely to be greater for the latter.

[48] Curiously, the opportunities for transfer pricing and other tax planning mechanisms may in some cases reduce the extent of tax arbitrage: why bother to move actual money or assets when you can achieve the same results by artificial planning techniques? Paul Krugman, a Nobel-winning economist and New York Times columnist, has advanced this argument.

First – as observed above – tax arbitrage is likely to be more effective for some tax provisions than others. Undoubtedly there is strong pressure for countries to coordinate their rules with respect to (say) transfer pricing or the computation of the foreign tax credit, if only as a way to restrict the losses from tax arbitrage. Perhaps there is even some pressure for coordination of nominal and effective corporate tax rates. But this pressure is likely to be much weaker for individual and family taxes, still less so for the details of tax administration, adjudication and enforcement. Even for the first category it has proved extraordinarily difficult to achieve agreement, and the differences between countries have in some cases grown deeper with the passage of time. The continuing debates on transfer pricing, permanent establishment, and similar issues are an example of this problem. The BEPS problem is a further example.

Second, tax arbitrage creates incentives for divergence as well as convergence. It only takes one country or one combination of countries to create an international tax shelter. Barring a sudden turn toward World Government, there will always be an incentive for the next Netherlands Antilles, Ireland, or whoever it may be to adjust their rules precisely in order to be different from other nations and thereby attract additional investment. One can say that these are "outliers" and other countries are the "norm," but if the strategy is successful, they are no longer the outliers: others will follow them, or else the larger countries will have to adjust their strategies in response.

Finally, tax arbitrage – even if it proves to be a powerful force for convergence – would be subject to the same political, social, and ideological factors that have historically frustrated previous convergence schemes.

An interesting perspective on tax arbitrage is provided by Reuven Avi-Yonah in his article "Tax Competition, Tax Arbitrage, and the International Tax Regime."[49] The central argument of the paper is that there exists a coherent international tax regime, embodying the single tax concept (i.e., the avoidance of double taxation) and the so-called benefit principle (income should be taxed where it provides the most economic benefit), which is consistent over time and between different countries. The paper recognizes that tax competition and tax arbitrage place substantial pressure on this system and that these pressures are as a general rule increasing with the passage of time. The coherence of the system is thus occasionally honored in the breach. But the international tax system has so far been able to resist these pressures and maintain the underlying principles described above.

Based on these observations, Avi-Yonah concludes that international tax is, in essence, simply another form of international law: it remains subject to the decisions and even the occasional whims of individual actors, but this does not mean that no

[49] University of Michigan Law School, Public Law and Legal Theory Working Paper No. 73 (January 2007), https://ssrn.com/abstract=955921.

principles exist, or that these principles will not survive the inevitable exceptions and derogations from them.

At bottom, the arbitrage argument is really a restatement of the broader case for globalization: that increased economic and cultural contact will inevitably bring countries closer together in legal and other matters. So far, this hasn't happened, or has happened only sporadically and inconsistently. Rephrasing the argument for globalization in economic rather than political terms serves to give it a superficial sense of inevitability, but it does not change the underlying reality. Change comes slowly, and sometimes not at all.

## 4.6 IS THERE A "GLOBAL TAX CULTURE," AND SO WHAT IF THERE IS?

To sum up, the process of globalization is arguably more advanced in tax than in other areas because of the technical nature of the subject; the relatively high degree of interaction among tax practitioners and policy-makers; and the proliferation of cross-border transactions, which both create economic pressure for conformity and contribute to the broadening of human contacts that can put such conformity in practice. But the process remains uneven and to some degree erratic in nature. Globalization, or (what amounts to largely the same thing) convergence, is more advanced for business than for individual taxes; for smaller than for larger countries; for lawyers, economists, and other tax professionals than for the average taxpayer. Harmonization of rules and practices has proven difficult even within geographic regions that share longstanding traditions, like Europe or North America, and will no doubt prove even more so on a worldwide basis. Even apparent convergence may at times prove superficial in nature: both governments and private citizens are adept at using the same words to mean radically different things, in tax no less than in other policy areas. There are pressures for convergence but offsetting pressures in the opposite direction, as nations seek to attract business or achieve domestic political goals by distinguishing themselves from their competitors. Which of these competing factors wins out in any given case is difficult and even hazardous to predict.

A similar skepticism should greet the concept of a "global tax culture." Such a culture definitely exists in the classrooms of international tax programs or the corridors of international tax organizations. It is likewise true that tax experts in different countries use remarkably similar language in discussing local tax issues. But this does not mean that national differences are unimportant, any more than the existence of the United Nations, or the fact that its members all use terminology like "freedom" and "democracy," means that they are all on the same playing field.

To be sure, globalization of business has engendered an increase in tax cooperation, so that tax policy is more global today than it was a generation ago. But how far this culture has descended into day-to-day tax decision-making remains an open question. Indeed, tax lags behind several other areas in international cooperation – trade, intellectual property, and perhaps even environmental law come to mind – and, as suggested above, it is not even clear that it is converging rather than diverging with the passage of time. The relative decline in power of the United States, and the rise of other countries (most notably China) with very different worldviews, suggests that these centrifugal forces may become still more significant in the near future.

Rather than a global tax culture, it seems more accurate to say that a sort of global subculture exists among tax academics, lay experts, and fiscal policy-makers, which coexists with a series of still distinct national tax cultures and interacts uneasily with them. Which of these cultures "wins out" in particular cases depends upon the country, the issue, and the timing of the clash in question. There is an ebb and flow in the competition between global and national cultures rather than a unitary movement in one direction.

None of this should be surprising or even especially disconcerting. It amounts simply to a recognition that people and ideas change slowly, especially when core beliefs about law, justice, and a good society are at stake. A subculture that exists in the halls of sophisticated institutions is an important phenomenon, but it is not a substitute for the honest recognition of differences between people, cultures, and geographic regions. Indeed, that subculture itself may be more a thinly veiled example of one particular national culture than a genuinely neutral or universal meeting place, even if this is sometimes less obvious to people who grew up in the dominant culture. We ignore these points at our peril.

The discussion to this point has been necessarily generic in nature, attempting to delineate broad themes that apply to the study of tax and culture in general. The remaining chapters will apply this framework to more specific problems. Chapter 5 considers the tax cultures of a number of countries and regions, including the Nordic region, China and India (again), and Israel, circling back to a reconsideration of American tax culture in light of the experience of these other nations. Chapter 6 considers the convergence or divergence of tax law in a number of distinct policy areas – tax progressivity, tax shelters/tax evasion, and environmental or carbon taxes – and examines the differences between them. Chapter 7 combines the insights of previous chapters into a series of useful and practical conclusions.

# 5

# Case Studies I: The Tax Cultures of Selected Western and Non-Western Countries

Culture, almost by definition, is hard to appreciate in the abstract. Sooner or later one must get one's hands dirty and do a certain amount of field work: the "thick description" that many speak of, but fewer have the opportunity to do. In the tax world, this consists less of tribal ceremonies and more of visits to tax agencies, law firms, and other outposts of modern tax practice and administration. While all of these places have some things in common – I have yet to see a genuinely cheerful tax office – there are enough differences to be worth a brief tour.

This chapter considers the tax cultures of selected countries and regions, emphasizing the issues (values, institutions, the influence of global or transnational actors) that were identified in previous chapters. There is no particular pattern to the places chosen, except that they happen to be places I have visited or of which I have at least a passing knowledge of the background language and culture.[1] I attempted to achieve geographic balance by emphasizing two European (Scandinavia and Italy), two Asian (China and India), and one hybrid tax culture (Israel). These sections are supplemented by briefer discussions of several other countries including Japan, Brazil, and Russia/Eastern Europe, the last particularly interesting because of its post-Marxist heritage and its (closely related) affinity for flat, nonprogressive income taxes. The chapter also includes a brief discussion of taxation and religion, an issue of particular importance in the Islamic world but also significant in several other regions, even when those living there do not always appreciate it.

The chapter concludes with a brief reconsideration of American tax culture in the light of the countries studied above. Although we have previously discussed this issue, there are many things that one cannot appreciate about one's own culture until one has lived somewhere else.[2] Notwithstanding its reputation as a world

[1] I must confess to being defeated by Chinese: by the end of my visit I was reduced to pointing to *zhe ge* (this one) or *nei ge* (that one) in restaurants and similar locales. For this reason I rely somewhat more heavily on secondary sources for China. The Nordics all spoke better English than I do, so this was not a big issue there. I am reasonably fluent in Hebrew and Italian.

[2] Calling to mind the famous story of the young Englishman who was asked about his experience after spending a year in France. I didn't learn much about France, he said, but many things about England.

leader, we will find the United States to be something of an outlier in several aspects of its tax culture, and becoming more so in some aspects.

## 5.1 BACKGROUND: LEGAL FAMILIES AND THEIR APPLICATION TO TAX LAW

Before reaching individual countries, it may be useful to say a word about the classification of legal and tax systems in general. The division of the world into legal "families" is as old as comparative law itself. The classic division was that of common law and civil law jurisdictions, the former including the English-speaking countries and their former colonies and the latter including continental Europe and its possessions together with those areas (notably Latin America) with which it maintained historic ties. There were always anomalies in this system, including places where civil and common law overlapped (Quebec, South Africa), others that borrowed from both systems (e.g., Japan), and some, like China, that seemed outside the Western system altogether. New categories were created to accommodate these anomalies, most notably socialist law, which was said to encompass the Soviet Union and its satellites, and religious or "traditional law," which was said to coexist with Western law in India, Africa, and other places that had been incompletely assimilated into the Western tradition. A typical corollary of this approach was the notion that Western law was superior to or more advanced than that of other regions, although this view is less common today.[3]

Because tax (and especially income tax) law is largely a twentieth-century product, the distinction between civil and common law is only partially applicable to it. This is not to say that it is wholly irrelevant. For example, the American emphasis on tax adjudication relates at least in part to its common law heritage, along with its tradition of judicial review or (as its critics would describe it) judicial lawmaking. China's traditional preference for administrative decisions and its more recent communist heritage undoubtedly have a similar effect on its tax behavior. Certainly the study of tax law is different in civil and common law jurisdictions. But these are broad distinctions that are hard to apply to specific tax outcomes.

A more meaningful classification would consider the sources of tax law in each country and the external influence upon them. Emphasizing these factors we might arrive at the following categories:

***American-influenced systems*** – These include the United States, Canada, much of the remaining Western hemisphere, and arguably Japan, which has a hybrid legal system but whose tax law was originally American-drafted.[4] While many of the countries have very different tax rules from the United States, the American influence remains strong on their institutional structure and categories of thought

[3] An example is Harold J. Berman, *Law and Revolution: The Formation of the Western Legal Tradition* (Cambridge: Harvard University Press, 1983).

[4] The Shoup Commission and its influence on Japanese tax law are discussed in Section 6.

on tax issues. Given the outsized American role in the global tax system, this group overlaps with several other categories.

***European Union*** – This would include the larger Western European states (France, Germany, etc.) as well as several smaller nations. For historic reasons, the Eastern European states arguably merit a separate category (see below). The Nordic nations, which have a somewhat ambiguous relationship with the EU, are likewise a special case.

***Post-Communist States*** – This group includes Russia and most, although not all, of its former Eastern European satellite countries, together with some non-European nations. These nations are distinguished by an aversion to progressive taxation and a rather less developed tax administration than their Western European peers. The historic lack of trust in government, with its inevitable effect on the level of tax compliance, is a further complicating factor.

***Former British Territories*** – Notwithstanding their many differences, countries like Israel, India, and other former British possessions share many elements of tax culture resulting from the creation of tax laws and institutions in the colonial period. Similar patterns apply in the French and other European colonial empires.

***Developing World*** – This is a tricky category because it is so broad. Two distinguishing factors are the relatively undeveloped nature of tax administration and the influence of international organizations, notably the IMF, on domestic tax policies. This category overlaps with the colonial and post-communist categories described above.

***China*** – In its own league, here as elsewhere (see discussion later in this chapter).

***Islamic countries*** – Part of the developing world, but with enough unique issues to merit its own separate category. The question of tax and religion is especially important in these nations, as we will discuss later on.

This list is presented primarily to provoke discussion and suggest the difficulty of classifying world tax systems by geography or other means. Having presented it, I shall proceed largely to ignore it, discussing more than one country from some categories (e.g., Europe), largely ignoring others, and including some places, like India, that overlap different categories. I will also take several detours on questions like Chinese culture, Islamic law, and other subjects.

## 5.2 HIGH TAXES AND HIGH TECHNOLOGY: THE TAX CULTURE OF THE NORDIC COUNTRIES

It is a truism of tax policy that taxes cannot be separated from spending or tax decisions from broader fiscal policy. Nowhere is this more evident than in the Nordic countries.[5]

[5] These are usually defined to include Sweden, Norway, Denmark, and Finland, and sometimes Iceland as well. Nordic tax culture was mentioned briefly in Chapter 3; this is a longer discussion.

The generous welfare states that characterize these countries are funded by equally high taxes and a very particular approach to tax administration, which has attracted interest even in geographically distant regions.[6] While Nordic tax systems are often thought to reflect deeply held "progressive" values, many of their most distinguishing features are of surprisingly recent origin, and popular attitudes have often followed institutional developments rather than the other way around. There are also substantial differences between the individual Nordic countries in tax and other matters, some of which have actually increased in recent years: they are similar less in political essence than in the mental framework they have adopted for dealing with tax and other public policy issues.

Three principal features characterize the Nordic tax approach. The first is high and only modestly progressive taxes on individual income, with middle-tier wage earners, and not only the rich, paying taxes at a relatively high marginal rate.[7] The second is low or at least lower taxes on corporate, dividend, and capital gain income, so that the countries in question derive a relatively high percentage of revenues from individual taxes and a relatively modest although not insignificant portion from taxes on business enterprise. This combination seems odd to American ears, which are used to equating tax fairness with higher taxes on corporations and other business concerns. but it has a certain logic in the Nordic countries, which are relatively small in size and remain heavily export-oriented, and have long combined domestic welfare states with aggressive promotion of their own local businesses.

A third characteristic is an unusually efficient system of tax administration, which relies heavily on computerized return filing and a "service" approach to taxpayers, and appears to achieve a relatively low level of tax avoidance. (Heavily regulated economies, and a preference for noncash transactions, also contribute to high compliance.) Like the first two features, this aspect differs between individual countries, but they remain consistent enough that it makes sense to speak of a common approach. Other aspects of Nordic taxation, including a growing reliance on carbon and other environmental taxes, are characteristic of one or more countries but as of yet are not part of the core model.[8]

When outsiders discuss Nordic taxes their first question is usually "how do they put up with it?" That is, how do people in democratic countries accept such high marginal tax rates?[9] One answer is that taxes are only a part of the question. The so-called

6 The classic work on welfare states generally is GØsta Esping-Andersen, *The Three Worlds of Welfare Capitalism* (Princeton University Press, 1990). A useful study of Nordic welfare states is Mary Hilson, *The Nordic Model: Scandinavia Since 1945* (London: Reaktion Books, 2011).

7 For example, Sweden has a maximum individual income tax rate of about 60 percent with an aggregate 50-percent rate reached at 468,700 kronor or about $47,000. By contrast, the corporate rate is only 22 percent and capital gain is taxed at a flat 30 percent. Rates in other countries vary but follow a similar pattern.

8 Environmental taxes are discussed further in Chapter 6.

9 See Henrik Jacobsen Kleven, "How Can Scandinavians Tax So Much?," *Journal of Economic Perspectives*, 28 (4) (2014), 77–98.

Nordic Model, which has been the subject of seemingly endless papers and conferences, includes not only high taxes but high benefits – free or reduced cost education, retirement, health care, retirement, child care, and so forth – that are typically provided to everyone ("universal benefits") rather than being limited to specific income groups. Indeed, the combination of universal benefits with an underlying capitalist system was central to the model's appeal as a so-called third way between capitalism and socialism, an appeal which has at least partially survived the demise of the Soviet Union and its satellites.[10] According to this explanation, Nordics are not handing over money to the government, but engaging in a sort of "one-stop shopping" where college tuition, health insurance, retirement savings, and so forth can simply be paid all at once rather than in separate installments as in the United States or other countries. The small populations of the Nordic countries and the resulting involvement of citizens in decision-making are also cited as encouraging low levels of evasion and high taxpayer morale.

The explanation above is appealing but not entirely persuasive. Would Americans really accept tax rates in excess of 50 percent even in return for Nordic-style social benefits? What if they wanted to attend alternative schools or universities, or preferred to self-insure for health purposes? Would middle-class voters agree to subsidize their less prosperous fellow citizens, an important and enduring aspect of the Nordic Model? Such questions have led some observers to postulate on the presence of something older and deeper in the Nordic culture – a communal sense, a commitment to self-sacrifice, plain old conformity, and group loyalty – that leads the people of the region to comply with rules that others wouldn't accept. Some trace this spirit to the Lutheran Church or all the way back to the Vikings, who, when not breaking heads, were said to share their spoils in an egalitarian manner, although the evidence on this point is spotty.

Like the theories that Americans always hate taxes or Italians never follow rules, there is something to this speculation ... but not terribly much. In fact the Nordic welfare states date not to the Vikings but to the 1930s, and were enacted in response to practical problems, including labor unrest and the combined threats of the Soviet Union and Nazi Germany, rather than owing to deep cultural roots. It also seems likely that at least some "Nordic values" are a response to institutional factors rather than their immediate cause. For example, Nordic tax and welfare systems require a high number of wage earners, including men and women, to remain solvent: the original push for gender equity came at least partly for this reason. Environmentalism and energy conservation result partly from ideology but also from the reality of large and rather cold countries with potentially high energy costs. This does not mean that Nordic values are not deeply held, but rather that – as we have already seen elsewhere – they are frequently more conditional than first

10 An early appreciation was Marquis Childs, *Sweden: The Middle Way* (New Haven: Yale University Press, 1936).

appears and institutional changes frequently preceded attitudinal shifts rather than following upon them.

A significant part of the Nordic equation relates to local systems of tax administration. These tend to be rather advanced technologically, with a heavy reliance on computerized data that makes return filing easier and tax evasion, at least in theory, more difficult.[11] The Nordic tax agencies have also attempted in recent years to adopt a "service" orientation that seeks to cooperate with taxpayers rather than imposing tax rules upon them. When I visited the Danish tax administration in Copenhagen, I saw a room full of people answering taxpayer questions complete with charts and diagrams to keep track of their responses. In Stockholm I was given a hardcover book (in English) with handsome blue and gold graphics and bearing the title "From feared tax collector to popular service agency," which explains the *skatterverket*'s transformation and touts it as a model for other tax agencies. The Norwegian tax directorate was so informal that people came to work in T-shirts and ski jackets (this is, in fairness, something of a national uniform in Norway). How much this goodwill is shared by taxpayers is hard to say, but – whether because they like to pay taxes or because the system allows few opportunities for evasion anyway – it does appear that the Nordic countries have achieved a relatively high level of taxpayer morale and a relatively low level of evasion.

Could the Nordic tax culture be transferred to other countries? The problem is that it is hard to separate one aspect from another. As we have seen, Nordic tax culture involves several elements including high taxes and benefits, efficient tax administration, and a populace that (for whatever reason) appears to retain higher levels of trust and cooperation than exist in North America.[12] In theory it might be possible to imitate one of these features – say, efficient tax administration – without necessarily adopting the others. But the features are to a large degree interdependent. Swedish, Danish, and Norwegian tax officials are able to adopt a service orientation in part because of specialized training, but in part because taxpayers, who are accustomed to receiving a very high level of benefits, are already predisposed to see taxes in a less adversarial way. Various quirks of Nordic society, like the prevalence of noncash transactions and the high level of transparency in financial dealings, make tax enforcement easier and evasion more difficult. Some features, like small and (until recently) homogenous populations or the Nordics' somewhat unusual geographic situation, might prove difficult or impossible to transfer.

A degree of skepticism may also be in order regarding some of the more exaggerated claims for the Nordic Model. Nordic businesses like Skype, Lego, and IKEA have invested heavily in promoting an image of healthy, innovative, and socially progressive living. Some of this image inevitably carries over to public policy. Problems like brain drain or anti-immigrant sentiment – often rationalized

[11] The Panama Papers scandal, which suggested that some Nordics (together with many others) had stashed money in that country in order to avoid taxes, cast at least tangential doubt on this assertion.

[12] Kleven, "How Can Scandinavians."

by the argument that immigration will destroy the existing welfare state model – are liable to be overlooked. Tax avoidance may be higher than previously realized.[13] Indeed, there is some doubt whether the model is sustainable even within the Nordic region itself, given the degree of competition from other countries and the slow but steady transition from homogeneous to multicultural societies, a transition which is most advanced in Sweden but is increasingly an issue in its neighbors as well.

The Nordic experience thus provides a good example of the portability of tax cultures but also of its limitations. Tax attitudes and institutions are difficult to separate from those in other places and are frequently tied to historical and geographic conditions that are difficult to duplicate in new situations. Yet those conditions are often the result of earlier choices that were by no means predetermined, and may themselves have involved extensive borrowing from other countries or regions. Things that seem inherent or inevitable may have been much less so a century or even a generation ago. Cultures change, but they do so slowly, and along a winding, irregular, and somewhat unpredictable path.[14]

It should be noted that the Nordic Model is not monolithic and that, in the view of many, it is no longer really a model at all. Sweden has lowered its tax rates substantially in the last twenty years, under pressure from globalization, Europeanization (Sweden joined the EU in 1995), and (some would say) a misguided effort to appease business interests. Norway's oil revenues enabled it to fund welfare benefits while maintaining lower taxes than would otherwise be the case. Denmark sometimes makes a point of not doing whatever Sweden does. Put differently, the Nordic countries "export" tax and welfare concepts but also "import" these concepts from other countries, many of them far removed from the region, and they define themselves by reference to but also in contradistinction to their immediate neighbors. Culture is local, but it is also permeable: geography is only one of the many factors that go into it.

## 5.3 NORTHERN AND SOUTHERN EUROPE: A FURTHER NOTE ON THE EU

The Nordic experience suggests the persistence of local and regional models notwithstanding the globalization phenomenon. Notwithstanding two millennia of common history – and notwithstanding the EU – European tax cultures remain as different as the countries themselves. The most obvious example is the distinction between Western and Eastern Europe, the former of which regards socialism as benign or at worst misguided, and the latter of which tends to think of it as something approaching a four-letter word.[15] But there remain vast differences within Western

13 See Chapter 3.

14 See, e.g., Sven Steinmo, *The Evolution of Modern States: Sweden, Japan, and the United States* (Cambridge University Press, 2010).

15 The tax systems of the former Soviet bloc are discussed further below.

Europe as well. These include differences in taxpayer attitudes, tax institutions, and the broader legal system in which tax law operates.

A good example of the persistence of local differences is provided by the Italian tax system.[16] On the surface, Italy has a tax system not terribly different from its European neighbors. There is an individual income tax (IRPEF) with a maximum 43 percent rate and somewhat lower rates on dividends and capital gain; a corporate income tax; a VAT; and various regional taxes, although some of those have been reduced or eliminated. Tax law is administered by the *Agenzia delle Entrate*, the local equivalent of the IRS, with tax policy at a broader level made by the Ministry of Finance and, ultimately, the Italian Parliament. Tax law (*diritto tributario*) is a regular course in Italian law schools, although many tax professors are also engaged in private practice, and tax policy appears to be made more by economists and public policy experts than by tax lawyers. As in most civil law jurisdictions, students tend to study the Code and associated textbooks (*manuali*) rather than judicial decisions, although the influence of the latter has increased somewhat with the advent of online reporting. The role of the EU in the income and especially value added taxes is similar to other European countries.

On the surface, the Italian tax system does not look all that different from those of neighboring countries. The differences start when one looks beneath the surface at the actual, day-to-day functioning of the Italian tax system. Three particular features stand out.

First, Italy has a tradition of tax avoidance so broad as to be essentially institutionalized. The phenomenon is, or is at least thought to be, so widespread that the country regularly offers tax amnesties (*amnistie, condoni*) without penalty in order to increase its short-term revenues: one observer described timely tax payment as in essence a bet that there would be no amnesty within the designated period. The sources of this attitude are many and varied, and it is by no means unique in Europe, but it appears to be something of an extreme.

Second, and perhaps related, Italy has a highly politicized and polarized debate on tax policy, including appropriate tax levels, punishment of tax evaders, and other issues. Tax increases and (oddly) even tax reductions have been met by impassioned debates, street protests, and in one case a strike by forestry workers which threatened to bring an entire region to a halt. The politicization of taxes, together with the close proximity of countries (notably Switzerland) with somewhat better fiscal reputations, helps fuel the tax avoidance phenomenon, especially with regard to capital income.

Third, the Italian Republic has, for a variety of historical reasons, effectively constitutionalized a number of important tax rules, so that the debate on these rules becomes a matter of judicial as well as legislative or executive interest. Thus the idea of *capacita' contributiva* (variously translated as taxpaying

[16] This discussion, together with that of Israel and India, is drawn in part from my previous articles.

capacity or ability to pay), which is in most countries an academic concept, is in Italy a constitutional provision, although nobody seems quite sure exactly what it means. It was this provision that the Constitutional Court used to require separate returns by husbands and wives, a decision that substantially complicated the effort to achieve progressivity on a country-wide basis. (Two-earner couples tend to be wealthier on average, and single-earner couples poorer, especially those with more than one child.) The French and German constitutional courts have taken equally and sometimes more aggressive roles in tax matters.

Finally, there are several features of Italian society that impact the tax system less directly. The Italian economy retains a large sector of so-called family capitalism, companies like Gucci, Fendi, or Benetton providing a case in point. In a number of these enterprises the women provide the creative energy while the men serve as bankers, financiers, and so forth. (In some cases, the women do both.) Arrangements of this sort make it difficult or impossible to distinguish business from personal expenses, even if one is trying to do so honestly.

Italy also has huge regional differences, which it has tried to address by tax deductions or credits for regions, like Sicily and the South, and activities, like fishing or female-headed enterprises, which are historically underdeveloped. These provisions are politically attractive but also reduce tax revenues and have come under EU scrutiny as hidden subsidies to domestic enterprises. At the opposite extreme, business (and especially capital gain) income is concentrated in Milan and other northern cities, which are geographically and psychologically closer to Switzerland than the remainder of their own country. Higher tax rates on such income may simply result in the income being taken across the border, either by legitimate transactions or simple tax avoidance, with no resulting revenue gain. Put differently, the unique features of Italian society favor the development of special or unusual tax rules and unique interpretations of generally accepted principles, which may then have a different and surprising effect.

The Italian situation is perhaps extreme, but it is hardly unique. Every European country – the Nordics with their welfare state, Italy with its tradition of tax avoidance, Eastern Europe as it struggles with the legacy of communism – has its unusual, quirky features which affect tax policy and outcomes. The United Kingdom has a common law jurisprudence and an emphasis on individual rights that is markedly different from that on the continent. (This is one, although hardly the only, reason for the Brexit conundrum.) The Netherlands has a longstanding commercial tradition but also a reputation as something of a world capital of tax evasion. Germany has a constitutional court, and France a "constitutional council," that have interfered with tax policy in a way that would make even the US Supreme Court blush. These differences are significant even within the European region and become more so as one moves further abroad. Regional organizations and the rise of a "global tax culture" go only so far in restricting these developments.

## 5.4 THE LEGACY OF COLONIALISM AND A TRADITION OF TAX EVASION: NOTES ON ISRAELI TAX CULTURE

If the Nordic and Italian situation are two extremes within Europe, Israel is more complex situation. Like everything else in the country, Israeli tax culture is a hybrid, involving a mix of European, Middle Eastern, and Jewish aspects together with a generous helping of serendipity. Yet Israel – here as elsewhere – is not completely unique, but rather a more extreme case of a situation which is common in many countries, particularly younger nations with a colonial or neocolonial history .

To a large extent, the Israeli tax system was inherited from the British Mandate in Palestine (1922–48). As a colonial power, the British Government did not have to win local elections: its goal was to collect the necessary revenue in the most efficient manner with the lowest administrative cost. This was accomplished largely by imposing taxes on urban workers and allowing the informal rural economy to escape tax altogether. Since more Jews lived in the cities and more Arabs in the villages, this resulted in more tax being imposed on the Jews than the Arabs, although this appears to have been a matter of convenience than design. An unanticipated side effect was that, after independence, the Jews had a better revenue-raising system and thus more money to buy weapons from foreign sources than did the Arabs, one of many advantages that propelled them to victory in the 1948 and most subsequent conflicts in the region.[17]

The situation today is more complex, but some essential features remain. Israel continues to impose relatively high taxes on labor income, although marginal rates have been reduced in recent years and the top rates are reached more slowly than in the Nordic countries, especially when adjusted for average income levels. Perhaps more important, most of these taxes are withheld at the workplace, and many Israelis have historically filed no or relatively short tax returns, although this too is changing. By contrast, taxation of income from capital has historically been rather halfhearted: there was no tax on capital gain for many years and (somewhat amazingly) no effective tax on overseas income until more recently, and enforcement remains somewhat leaky in these and other areas.

Domestic Israeli businesses are subject to tax, but there is a relative lack of written rules and a widespread perception that small cash businesses (falafel stands, coffee bars, etc.) underreport their income to an extraordinary degree, a fact which may account for the seemingly incredible number of such businesses. A large public

[17] See generally Assaf Likhovski, *Tax Law and Social Norms in Mandatory Palestine and Israel* (Cambridge University Press, 2017).

sector, much of it tax exempt, and a large number of people supported by generous family allowances complicate matters further. The informality of the Israeli tax system places a premium on a relatively small number of well-connected tax lawyers, many of them former tax officials, who negotiate settlements on behalf of delinquent taxpayers, and are said to be successful at doing so.[18]

Although it appears to raise sufficient revenue, Israel's unusual tax culture has a distorting effect on its economy and society. Because tax rates on wages are high – and wages tend to be low by Western standards to begin with – it is virtually impossible to maintain a high standard of living by salary income alone. Instead, nearly every middle-class family has devised one method or another to obtain untaxed economic benefits. One family lives in an apartment that is provided rent-free by their parents, while another leases out rooms and asks to be paid only in cash. Others return home for the weekend loaded with fruits, vegetables, and other food provided by families or friends. Real estate lawyers, including some well-known figures, are compensated by a percentage of the transaction rather than by a fixed fee. There are of course nontax reasons for some of this, but it hard to avoid that, in a society which imposes high taxes on wages and leaky or no taxes on many other transactions, people tend to prefer the latter. This is before one even gets to the extensive income from overseas transactions, primarily in Europe or the United States, which are no longer tax-exempt but on which taxes are often lower and enforcement is likely to be leakier.

Given the country's egalitarian traditions – Israel was founded as a sort of Zionist commonwealth and socialists ran the government for the first thirty years – one might expect that taxes would be a major political issue. By and large, this has not been the case. Part of this results from the focus on security issues, which tends to push other problems to the side and to make raising them seem almost unpatriotic. A more cynical explanation is that people have simply gotten used to the system and no one has the energy or inclination to change it. Many programs that would be administered through the tax code in other countries, like assistance to poor families or credits for desired activities, are accomplished by direct spending programs in Israel, so that they are treated as expenditure rather than tax policy issues. Attitudes toward these problems frequently divide along ethnic or religious rather than economic lines and are settled by coalition politics rather than principled discussion. For example, the issue of family allowances has largely been subsumed in the question of the so-called ultra-orthodox (Haredi) community and its role in society.

In recent years there has been an effort to bring distributive justice (*tzedek khalukati*) back to the Israeli academic and political agenda.[19] This movement received its impetus from the so-called cottage cheese protest in Tel Aviv (Israeli dairy products are astronomically expensive) and helped gave birth to the Yesh Atid

[18] A useful if aging source is Harvey C. Wilkenfeld, *Taxes and People in Israel* (Cambridge: Harvard University Press, 1973).

[19] See, e.g., Menachem Mautner (ed.), *Tzedek Halukati B'Yisrael* (*Distributive Justice in Israel*), 2001.

(There Is a Future) party headed by Yair Lapid, a former TV personality whose father was a similarly offbeat politician.[20] So far this movement has emphasized other issues, but if it came to power it would be difficult for it to avoid tax policy altogether. More generally, as Israel worries less about survival and becomes a more "normal" country, its tax and other domestic policy debates may be expected to become more like those in other developed countries. For the moment, this appears to be some years off.

How does Israeli tax culture fit into the broader global framework? At first glance Israel appears to be something of an oddball case, involving a quasi-European society in a Middle Eastern setting. Yet in some respects it may actually be ahead of its time. A hybrid, Western-cum-non-Western culture is rapidly becoming the norm in many developing countries whose tax and other institutions were imported from someplace else and must coexist with older, local traditions. (India, discussed in Section 5, has similar if inevitably larger issues.) The distortion of society by uneven taxation and the tendency to see tax issues as an extension of nontax political problems are similarly widespread phenomena. Informal tax administration, with unwritten rules and a high degree of delegation to individual agents, is the norm in many countries. It may hurt Israelis to think so, but in these features their country is not really unique, but all too typical.

## 5.5 AUTHORITARIANISM, HARMONY, AND THE BHAGAVAD GITA: THE TAX CULTURES OF CHINA AND INDIA

Differences in culture always become more apparent the further one gets from home. Perhaps for this reason the very term "globalization" is enough to cause many non-Westerners to roll their eyes. The reason is obvious. For at least three centuries, "universal" standards have, in practice, meant Western standards in culture, technology ... and law. This is especially true in tax policy, which has to a significant degree been dictated by the United States, United Kingdom, and a few other countries. The degree to which issues are centered on the Western (and specifically English-language) perspective becomes apparent in conversation, where people will interrupt a lengthy stream of Italian, Hindi, or Chinese to say "transfer pricing" or "affiliated group" in English, as if the local equivalent, if there is one, could not possibly express the same concept. That these terms may not mean precisely the same thing in different languages, or that their superficial similarity may be overshadowed by much deeper cultural differences, is not always so readily observable.

20 Yesh Atid is now part of a broader, vaguely left-of-center coalition.

The rise of China and India poses a special challenge to Western hegemony, different in nature and degree from that of previous competitors. While the United States can to some degree dictate tax policy to its regional neighbors, and perhaps even to individual European countries, China is simply too big to let that happen. This is partly a matter of size and partly of philosophy: even the words for "rule of law" in Chinese (*fa zhi*) mean something different than in English, more closely approximating rule "by" rather than "of" legal rules.[21] (There is a difference.) It does not take very long in China to realize that virtually every legal concept takes on a different significance.

India presents a more subtle but potentially a more important challenge. While the Indian tax elite is superficially similar to that of many Western countries, it presides over a radically different culture and society, and its command of English language and legal principles suggests that it may remake those principles from the inside rather than posing an outside challenge. To put the matter more pithily, there is a conflict between Chinese and Indian culture, on the one hand, and the global tax culture on the other hand, and it is no longer reasonable to assume that this conflict will be resolved entirely in one direction.

This section considers the rise of China and India, and (to a lesser extent) other Asian countries, and its effect on the issues discussed in this book. The approach is, perhaps inevitably, impressionistic, emphasizing a small number of case studies rather than a comprehensive portrait of Chinese, Indian, or broader Asian culture. After considering each country separately, the chapter circles back to make a few broader points about the convergence of tax culture(s) and the limits of the globalization process, together with some insights about Western tax culture that become more readily apparent in a comparative spotlight.

### 5.5.1 *China*

As anyone who has been there knows well, going to China is more like visiting another planet than another country. Even today, the flight takes fourteen hours from the East Coast and – allowing for time zone changes – one arrives there a full day later than one left. Numerous writers, notably Simon Leys in his famous work *Chinese Shadows*, have described the distorting sense on one's perceptions: there is a tendency to suspend beliefs and accept nearly anything that one is told, even when it contradicts one's previously held positions or (at times) the evidence of one's own senses.[22]

Hyperbole aside, China is indeed different, in tax and other matters. Even on a short trip some of these differences become quickly obvious, while others require a somewhat more sustained analysis.

21 An interesting post on this point is Larry Catá Becker, "Fazhi in China: Rule of Law, Rule by Law: Rule Through Legal System," lcbackerblog.blogspot.com (April 30, 2013).

22 Simon Leys, *Chinese Shadows* (New York: Viking Press, 1977).

First, the Chinese have a very pronounced tendency to discuss things in group rather than individual terms. Progressive taxation, and redistribution in general, are discussed in terms of "harmony" (*he* or *he xie*) rather than in the Western terms of individual reward and punishment, diminished marginal utility, and so forth. While some of this is simply rhetoric, there is no question that the balance between individual and social goals is quite different than in a Western context. Sometimes these differences are less benign: there have been reports of people being shot for the crime of forging tax receipts, although such information can frequently be difficult to confirm.

Second, the Chinese have a different approach to the resolution of legal disputes than is common in the West, emphasizing the maintenance of relationships – and arguably of state power – more than the vindication of abstract rights. As Stanley Lubman describes in his book *Bird in a Cage*, this preference has roots in traditional Confucian society, but has been adopted by the communist or postcommunist state for its own purposes. Lubman views this difference as a unifying theme which explains many of the differences between the Chinese and Western approaches to law.[23]

In the tax field, the emphasis on relationships is manifested by a strong preference for the administrative rather than the judicial or legislative resolution of taxpayer disputes. Tax legislation tends to be rather vague and general in nature, and tax judicial decisions, at least at the national level, are relatively rare.

By contrast, the State Administration of Taxation (SAT), which occupies an enormous building in an outlying area of Beijing, often appears to be all-powerful, writing regulations, negotiating tax treaties, and resolving disputes at least some portion of which would be decided by the courts or the legislature in most other countries. For similar reasons – and perhaps to avoid uncomfortable human rights issues – Chinese tax officials tend to prefer dealing with accounting rather than law firms, especially where foreigners are concerned.

Third, and most obvious, China is enormous, subsuming provinces and even cities that are larger in population than many European countries. In a few more years it will be, if it isn't already, the largest economy in world history.[24] This size, and the enduring resentment of slights endured when it was weaker, result in an aggressiveness in tax and other matters that has no real parallel among other existing nations. When I asked a Chinese official if he was worried that higher tax rates might encourage foreign businesses to invest in Vietnam or similar countries instead, he smiled at me without even answering, the way an American might smile if I asked whether her country was afraid of being displaced by Cuba or the British Virgin Islands. That is not to say that the Chinese never cooperate in tax matters, particularly when they involve technical issues or when cooperation is necessary to protect

[23] Stanley Lubman, *Bird in a Cage: Legal Reform in China after Mao* (Stanford University Press, 2000).
[24] The precise ranking depends on whether nominal or adjusted (purchasing power) GDP is employed.

Chinese interests. But the dynamic is fundamentally different than with any other country, at least in the post-1945 era.

It must be added that, in addition to cultural differences, China has a unique political structure, combining an at least nominally socialist political philosophy with a growing, essentially capitalist economy. Chinese incomes are also distributed rather unevenly, with the more prosperous coastal provinces having per capita GDPs as much as ten times as high as the poorer inland areas, although this has changed somewhat in recent years. (This may also be one reason why the Chinese are skeptical about allowing free elections, even on a local basis.) Both tax institutions and the political playing field on which they operate are thus quite different from Western norms.

Writing meaningfully about Chinese taxes requires fluent Mandarin together with a rather sophisticated tax background, and accordingly there are few experts outside of China themselves. Perhaps the most provocative is Jinyan Li, who was born in China and teaches in Canada. Li's articles form a sort of roadmap of the Chinese tax system, as it adjusts to the world and simultaneously presses the world to adjust to it. In a 2010 article, Li uses the Chinese and Canadian antiavoidance rules (GAAR) as a case study in tax transfers and their limitations. While these rules are similar on paper, she finds that they diverge in practice because of the countries' different legal institutions, taxpayer attitudes, and definitions of tax avoidance.[25]

In a subsequent article, Li examines the reasons for this cultural divergence in more detail.[26] According to Li, the relevant differences consist less of substance than of procedure, including what she terms tax processes (legislation, administration, and dispute resolution) and transplantation processes (i.e., the selection of norms to be transplanted and their adaptation to prevailing local conditions). Perhaps not surprisingly, Li concludes that attempts to transfer substantive norms to another country without considering differences in either of these two different types of legal processes are likely to prove unsuccessful.

Another prominent scholar, Wei Cui, has written extensively on Chinese taxation in both English and Chinese. One of his principal concerns is the nature of Chinese tax decision-making and its effect on substantive outcomes. In an article titled "What Is the 'Law' in Chinese Tax Administration,"[27] he argues that informal rules have frequently had the force of law in China even when they appear to contradict decisions of higher authorities. The State Administration of Taxation issued a regulation designed to improve the transparency, clarity, and consistency of tax rulemaking, but its effects had not yet manifested themselves before Cui's paper was published. In another article he considers the role of judicial independence in authoritarian regimes, reaching the

25 "Tax Transplants and Local Culture: A Comparative Study of the Chinese and Canadian GAAR," *Theoretical Inquiries in Law*, 11 (2) (2010).

26 "Tax Transplants and the Critical Role of Processes: A Case Study of China," *Journal of Chinese Tax and Policy*, 3 (2013),85–139.

27 *Asia Pacific Law Review*, 19 (1) (2011).

somewhat surprising conclusion that – even when the judiciary is honest and competent – litigation may be ineffective if the rule of law is weak and potential litigants are unwilling to challenge state authority.[28]

### 5.5.2 *India*

If China is the paradigm of resistance to Western law, India might better be called the paradigm of the legal transplant. The word "hybrid" shows up so often in discussions of Indian law as to become somewhat repetitious. This is not to suggest that India is somehow weaker or less Asian than China: neither of these is, or will long be, the case. Rather, its history proceeded in a different fashion, a result of Hindu religious traditions, regional differences, and the continuing influence of the British Raj. Notwithstanding many changes, it remains quite different today, as even a short visit to the two countries will tell.

Perhaps the classic study of the Indian legal system is Marc Galanter's *Law and Society in Modern India*, originally published in 1989. A series of articles rather than a single monograph, the book emphasizes the British effort to impose a uniform legal system on the Indian subcontinent and the decidedly mixed success of that effort. The result is a patchwork system in which a largely anglicized judiciary administers an essentially anglicized law at a national level, but older traditions – themselves a mixture of Hindu, Muslim, and preexisting cultural norms – continue to hold sway in the villages and among less wealthy or well-educated citizens in the major cities.

This hybrid character, Galanter argues, persisted even where the British made a good faith effort to accommodate Indian traditions, because in administering (or attempting to administer) local traditions with British-style institutions, they inevitably anglicized those traditions and stripped them of much of their authentic local character. (For example, written precedents were central to British law, but much less so in the Indian tradition.) Indeed, the very idea of "Indian" as opposed to Hindu or provincial law was largely a British creation. A similar process occurred in other British colonies: India was simply bigger, more complicated, and more important in nature, and therefore a more compelling example of this development.[29]

Tax is a very particular area of law, and what applies to law generally may not always be relevant to tax. Still, much of Galanter's analysis remains applicable to the Indian tax system. At a superficial level, it does indeed resemble the tax system of a European nation, with similar taxes (progressive income tax, VAT, assorted local levies) and a similar discourse at the higher levels of government, academia, etc. That a significant number of Indian tax officials have attended American or

28 "Does Judicial Independence Matter? A Study of the Determinants of Administrative Litigation in an Authoritarian Regime," *University of Pennsylvania Journal of International Law*, 38 (3) (2016), 941–998.

29 Marc Galanter, *Law and Society in Modern India* (Oxford University Press, 1989).

European tax programs contributes further to this similarity. The British traditions of Indian law and of the Indian upper class generally – cricket is the national sport and schoolboys may be observed playing rugby in Delhi and Mumbai (Bombay) – contribute further to this sometimes false sense of familiarity, as does the widespread use of English in national tax policy-making, less to appease foreigners than because many southern Indians speak English better than Hindi.

The problem starts when one looks below the surface at the actual functioning rather than the superficial design of the Indian tax system. Here, a number of differences become apparent. The first is the astonishing diversity of India, which means that the same rules have a different significance than they would in a Western country. For example, the national ("Union") income tax kicks in at a level of 250,000 rupees (about $3,500) per year, which means that a relatively small percentage of Indians – primarily wage earners in the larger cities (Mumbai, Delhi, Bangalore, etc.) – actually pay the tax. This, in turn, makes the income tax (as in China) account for a relatively small share of national revenues, arguably more akin to the estate tax in the United States than our own income levy, and increases reliance on other, less progressive taxes. As incomes rise this will change, but it is an example of superficially similar laws having a radically different significance in a different economic and cultural environment.

The size and relative backwardness of India, at least outside the large cities, also demand a different style of tax administration. Since relatively few people file tax returns, tax officials have been forced to looked for secondary indicia – ownership of a car, possession of a cell phone, and so forth – to identify potential taxpayers. It has been reported that a percentage tax on business turnover was abandoned because shop owners did not understand the percentage concept, although this story may well be apocryphal. (People frequently claim not to understand things that would cost them money.) All this is typical for developing nations, but in India it coexists with a population of 50 or 100 million people living a more or less European lifestyle, a situation without precise parallel elsewhere.

The colonial tradition in India also has a curiously mixed effect. In theory, it would produce Western values and a Western sense of efficiency. In practice, it left a hodgepodge of often irrational rules and practices. In Chapter 2 I mentioned the rule, a leftover from colonial days, that agricultural income may be taxed only by the state (regional) and not by the Union government. It did not take long for lawyers to devise tax shelters that involved the shifting of urban income to "agricultural" areas, sometimes located just outside the major cities – a sort of internal transfer pricing that results in substantial tax evasion. Tax evasion in general appears to be something of a national sport: in a bookstore in Mumbai I saw several books with titles like "Beat the Taxman" and suggesting numerous schemes, some legitimate and some perhaps less so, for reducing personal and business taxes. For their part, tax officials are under enormous pressure to produce revenues and have inherited at least some of the colonial contempt for their subjects: stories of their vindictiveness and even cruelty toward taxpayers are legendary.

The role of lawyers deserves further mention. Lawyers' time is relatively cheap in India, and taxpayers are constantly being challenged on relatively small items, like the deductibility of drivers employed for allegedly business purposes. (Everyone of any consequence in India has a driver, a fact that will be easily understood by anyone who has tried to drive there.) The result is a virtually endless flow of litigation, frequently intended to delay more than to avoid the actual tax payment. In Bombay I met with a group of tax lawyers late on a Friday afternoon, assuming that this was their final meeting of the day. I was a bit surprised when all of them returned to their offices to prepare additional cases. In this area, at least, India is rather the opposite of China: a highly litigious, argumentative society in which individual rights are protected to an extraordinary degree but economic and political efficiency are often at a loss.

While lawyers spend a great deal of time litigating, they are somewhat less influential with respect to Indian tax policy. Indeed, I was surprised to learn that tax is not even a regular course in most Indian law schools. The big-picture decisions tend to be left to economists or policy experts, with a nonpartisan think tank on the outskirts of Delhi playing a particularly important role. (Think tanks in general are popular in the country.) Whether this has to do with Indian traditions or is simply an institutional quirk, dating from time of the British Raj, is difficult to determine.

The issues above are practical in nature and might arise in any developing country. But there is also a deeper, philosophical level on which India is different. Global, which is really to say Western, tax policy is discussed almost exclusively in utilitarian, result-oriented terms. Fairness, efficiency, and simplicity or administrability are all essentially utilitarian concepts, even if this usually goes without notice. These concepts can at times be difficult to express in a culture whose primary texts lie outside this tradition, and indeed to some degree are the negation of it. Even today, and even among Western-educated Indians, these differences remain noticeable.

Perhaps the classic expression of Indian thought, the Bhagavad Gita, suggests that people get into trouble precisely when they seek rewards for good conduct rather than engaging in right conduct for its own sake – about as direct a refutation of the "utility" concept as one is likely to find anywhere in the world. (The Gita also suggests that people should not marry outside their own caste, but that's another story.) This difference is admittedly more subtle than the individual/collective dichotomy observed in China, and its effect on Indian tax professionals, who have a largely Western-style training, is probably indirect at best. But there remains a certain quality to Indian thought, which may be called "wisdom" or "fatalism" depending on one's mood and perspective, that can be difficult to express in Western terms. Together with the sheer magnitude of the country, it may result in a certain incomprehension on the part of foreign observers, who cannot understand why India would remain so far "behind" China or Japan in economic or political matters and why Indians persist in honoring traditions and values that have long since been abandoned in the West. Part of the answer may be that the terms "ahead" and "behind" themselves carry substantial cultural baggage.

The contrast between China and India suggests that the "Asian challenge" is by no means monolithic in nature. Indeed, the two are in many respects opposites, China highly centralized and authoritarian in nature and India suffering from a surfeit, if such a thing is possible, of democracy and (most especially) of lawyers. The underlying Hindu and Confucian philosophies are as different as the American and Russian systems of thought, perhaps more so.[30] Yet both countries see things in fundamentally different ways from the West, and both have the power and influence to compel others to begin seeing things their way as well. For the United States, which is used to dealing with countries that are a fraction of its size and power, confronting such large and assertive countries is a radically new and different experience.

Because India is less economically powerful than China – and perhaps because its differences are more subtle in nature – it has not yet challenged the global tax system in the way that China has. Yet the challenge that it poses may be no less important. It is said in India that the country has a history of swallowing foreign invaders: the Aryans, the Moghuls, the British, the Americans, and so on. Someday, it is said, we will all speak English with an Indian accent, eat Indian foods, accept the superiority of Indian philosophy and religion, and so on. Perhaps someday the problems that face the Indian tax system – hybrid rules, historical quirks, a large and seemingly irreducible gap between the rules applying to the elites and the masses – will be our problems as well. For now, it is sufficient to say that Indian tax culture remains quite different from that existing in Western and even other non-Western countries, and a superficially similar set of rules, even when written in English, does little to reduce that difference.

## 5.6 OTHER IMPORTANT JURISDICTIONS: JAPAN, THE BRICS COUNTRIES, AND THE ISLAMIC WORLD

China and India are of course not the only Asian countries, or for that matter the only developing countries, in the global arena. Many of the smaller "dragon" economies (Korea, Taiwan, Singapore, and the various nations of Southeast Asia) share several features with China, including authoritarian tendencies, an emphasis on the collective rather than the individual, and a historic preference for administrative rather than judicial resolution of disputes, in taxation and other matters. Recent history has likewise left these

30 See Michael D. Coogan, *Eastern Religions: Confucianism, Shinto, Hinduism, Buddhism, Taoism* (Oxford University Press, 2005).

countries with a profound distaste for the imperiousness of the Western powers even when they are politically and strategically allied to them. For the moment, these countries are too small to challenge the West directly, and their fear of Chinese dominance makes them reluctant to ally themselves too closely with their more powerful neighbor. With the passage of time this will very likely change, and Western dominance will be a thing of the past in tax policy as it is in other matters.

Japan is a fascinating and arguably a unique case. In law as in other matters it is a complex, hybrid culture, mixing Asian traditions with British, European, and more recently American norms that were added – some Japanese say imposed – after 1945.[31] Language and culture render the Japanese legal system, together with other aspects of the country, largely impenetrable to all but a small number of Western experts who have devoted substantial time and energy to the subject.

The American influence is particularly strong in the tax field. The so-called Shoup Mission, led by the American economist Carl Shoup in 1949, rewrote the Japanese tax system to bring it in line with American tax law, or – it is perhaps more accurate to say – the law that American tax experts would have liked to draft in the United States if domestic politics had permitted. (A similar role was played by British tax experts in crafting Israeli, Indian, and other colonial tax laws.) A colorful figure said to have ridden his horse to high school in California, Shoup also had substantial influence on the tax codes of Canada and several Latin American countries and is regarded as the intellectual father of the value added tax. The Shoup Mission was part of a much larger remaking of Japanese law, politics, and culture on the part of the (predominantly American) occupation forces, although one in which the Japanese themselves played a more substantial role than is generally recognized: the preservation of the Japanese monarchy, by no means a safe assumption during the war years, is perhaps the best known example of this influence.[32]

At first glance the Japanese tax system is not terribly different from that of the United States or other advanced countries. There is an individual income tax at rates ranging from 5 to 45 percent, the latter kicking in at 40 million yen (about $370,000), together with local taxes that raise the aggregate rate by up to 10 percent. There is a corporate tax at a rate of approximately 31 percent, a reduction from over 50 percent in the mid-1990s and 40 percent or more for much of the surrounding period. Capital gain is generally treated similarly to other income, subject to special rules for certain real property and (for individuals only) the sale of corporate shares. There is additionally a VAT (currently 8 percent), an inheritance tax, and several other levies. Taxes are administered by the National Tax Agency (NTA) under the supervision of the Ministry of Finance, in a manner not terribly different from the

[31] For a comprehensive treatment of the postwar occupation of Japan and the (frequently uneasy) interaction of American and Japanese values, see John W. Dower, *Embracing Defeat: Japan in the Wake of World War II* (New York: W.W. Norton & Co., 2000).

[32] Ibid.

American IRS and Treasury Department. Also like the United States, Japan has a fairly constant series of tax reforms, including one scheduled for 2019: as in the American case, the majority of these reforms appear to involve largely incremental changes, especially to business taxes, rather than structural overhauls.

Yet differences in legal and business culture mean that actual practice, as opposed to written tax law, remains quite different in the two countries, a difference that has generally expanded as Japan regained its independence and self-confidence in the intervening years.[33] For example, American executives frequently return from Japan believing they have received acquiescence to specific proposals whereas their hosts were merely too polite to contradict them directly. (This phenomenon is not limited to tax matters.) The allocation of tax decision-making authority is also rather different than in the United States, with internal appeals at the NTA having particularly great significance, and judicial decisions – although commanding a certain degree of respect – generally not treated as having a formal precedential value.

Japan is an interesting case study in the degree to which cultural differences make similar or even identical rules or practices take on different significance in different countries, and how this difference sometimes tends to expand rather than contract with the passage of time. The hybrid nature of legal systems is especially important here. Civil law traditions, traditional Japanese culture, and the aftereffects of occupation result in a system having no precise parallel elsewhere in the world.[34]

The challenges outside Asia are more diffuse but no less important. The remaining BRICS countries (Brazil, Russia, and South Africa) are perhaps the most obvious examples.[35] Both Brazil and South Africa are regional powers that view taxation as one part of their economic development and see themselves as spokespersons for their respective continents. The continuing concentration of wealth in one segment of each country's population – largely although not exclusively white in both cases – gives the issue of redistribution special force, although it also makes it more difficult to achieve by purely tax measures. In South Africa particularly there has been a tendency to use affirmative action – given local history, rather less controversial than the North American version – rather than tax policy as a way of redressing historic injustices. (India practices a form of affirmative action involving caste and ethnic group rather than an American conception of race as well.) Distributional issues have been highly controversial in both countries, although the reaction has been somewhat different, Brazil taking a sharp right turn with the recent election of

[33] The differences in Japanese and American business practices, particularly in the financial field, are described in great detail in Annelise Riles, *Collateral Knowledge: Legal Reasoning in the Global Financial Markets* (University of Chicago Press, 2011).

[34] See generally C. Milhaupt & J. Ramseyer, *The Japanese Legal System: Cases, Codes and Commentary* (2nd ed., 2012). A good source on taxes is Hiromishu Ishi, *The Japanese Tax System* (Oxford University Press, 2001).

[35] BRIC is an acronym for Brazil, Russia, India, and China, sometimes rendered BRICS to include South Africa also. I have considered China separately and discuss the remaining countries here.

Jair Bolsonaro as President and South Africa continuing on a more moderate path but subject to numerous controversies involving corruption, violence, and the continuing role of the African National Congress (ANC).

Brazilian tax policy reflects European and North American influence but also the country's internal politics, which has struggled to achieve a stable democracy since the country's emergence from dictatorship in the 1980s. (Bolsonaro's election is merely the most recent example of this problem.) Perhaps because of this instability, Brazilian taxation has a reputation for being extraordinarily complex, with allegations that Brazilian tax returns are the world's most difficult to complete. A study organized by Forbes Magazine found that tax professionals spent an average of 2,600 hours a year keeping up with the various Brazilian tax codes, more than twice as long as neighboring Bolivia and three or four times as long as the average country studied.[36] To what extent this phenomenon reflects a cultural tendency toward inefficiency on the one hand, and to what extent an institutional discontinuity created by frequent changes of regimes on the other, is a hard question to answer. The country's federal structure – something like the United States but with more power distributed at the regional level – has also made tax policy especially difficult to coordinate. Other Latin American countries, although for the most part rather smaller than Brazil, have faced similar issues.

One interesting aspect of South African taxation is the country's role as a sort of tax mentor to other African nations. This takes the form of structured endeavors, like the African Tax Institute (ATI), and less formal partnerships on the part of South African universities and government agencies. The South African role is significant, because many African nations have historically been forced to accept "advice" from the IMF and similar non-African organizations, which are frequently high-handed in approach and have not always had the continent's best interests at heart. The South African efforts are, in part, an attempt to redress this imbalance. That said, not all African nations accept South African leadership willingly, and there is at least some backlash against the country's efforts to influence its regional neighbors.

Russia and the neighboring Eastern European countries present another special case. Because of their unhappy experience with communism, these countries tend to be suspicious of anything that smacks of redistribution and were, until recently, somewhat overly credulous regarding capitalist development. Not by accident, these are among the few countries to maintain flat, or nearly flat, income taxes, although there have been proposals for change. For example, Russia taxes income at a flat 13 percent for residents and 30 percent for nonresidents, with a flat 15-percent rate on dividend income, about as flat a system as one is likely to see in the real world. Hungary and the Czech Republic also have flat (proportional) income taxes,

[36] Joe Harpaz, "Brazil Ranked Most Time-Consuming Tax Regime in the World," *Forbes* www.forbes.com (December 17, 2013).

although their tax systems differ in other ways from the Russian model. Other post-Soviet countries have by and large similar systems.[37]

The region's turbulent history also affects taxation in less positive ways, especially in the former Soviet republics. There is a profound lack of confidence in tax administration together with a tendency to abuse tax and other institutions for political purposes, two phenomena that are of course closely related to each other. This is particularly true since communist nations frequently lack a full-fledged, modern tax system, so that tax administration is often less than a generation old in these countries. (Taxation is complicated when most income-producing assets are, at least in theory, owned by the state or state-controlled enterprises.) For this reason, much of the research on taxpayer culture/compliance and how to change it focuses on the post-communist nations.

A fascinating case is presented by Estonia, which was incorporated into the Soviet Union but also has historic ties to Sweden, Finland, and the Baltic region. (The name "Estonia" derives from its earlier status as an eastern province of Sweden.) The country has a flat 21-percent individual, corporate, and capital gain income tax, a property tax on land but not buildings, and a "territorial" tax on international transactions that effectively exempts foreign profits from taxation. There is also an EU-compliant 20-percent VAT with reduced rates on medical and other products and a high level of electronic filing throughout the system. Put differently, Estonia has a tax system that has some features typical of Eastern Europe but others that reflect a Scandinavian character together with the influence of international tax experts. The combination has earned Estonia the title of the OECD's most competitive tax system – an improbable achievement for a small country that regained its independence barely thirty years ago.

Estonia – and Eastern Europe in general – suggest the difficulty of classifying tax or legal systems by any single factor alone. The tax systems in this region are a unique combination of political, historical, and geographical features, leavened by the influence of the EU and the role of "enlightened" international opinion. Not all of these influences have been salubrious: one suspects that, with the passage of time, the countries in this region may lose some of their aversion to redistribution and become less different from the countries surrounding them. Some of the outcome may depend on the political struggle between a resurgent Russia, on the one hand, and the United States and its allies on the other. From this perspective, convergence is a highly contingent process: tax policies may well oscillate between different poles, depending on the interplay of external and internal forces, rather than moving inexorably toward a single norm. As Zhou Enlai reportedly said of the French Revolution, it remains too early to tell.

A word must be reserved for the Islamic world, which has occupied so much political attention in recent years. On the surface the tax systems of these countries

37 Poland has a mildly progressive, two-bracket system.

are not terribly different from those of other postcolonial jurisdictions in the kinds of taxes imposed or basic norms of tax administration. Most have income and value added taxes that are not superficially different from those of other similarly situated countries. (Israel and Iraq have improbably similar tax histories, together with several African countries, reflecting the longstanding British influence in these nations and the circumstances of their independence.)[38]

Below the surface, things get more interesting. Part of the difference relates to specifically Islamic taxes like the *zakat* or poor tax, sometimes translated as "alms" but considered a religious obligation and more equivalent to a tax in Western terms, which remains popular among several historically Islamic countries. But Islamic principles also affect the administration and interpretation of more conventional, Western-style levies. For example, interest payments continue to be illegal in certain jurisdictions, or must at least be called by another name. The vocabulary for arguing tax issues may also be different, without a clear line between religious and secular ideals, or no real concept of a secular sphere at all.[39] To a certain extent, this may amount to similar arguments with different labels, but (as in China) the use of different language sooner or later results in different substantive outcomes. As these countries drift further from the West in their overall legal systems, these differences are likely to multiply.

The tax system of Pakistan, India's neighbor and its historic rival, is an interesting case in point. Like India, Pakistan has a progressive income tax that is paid by a relatively small percentage of the country's population and has similar issues of tax administration and evasion. Like India, many of the country's tax practices originated during the British Raj. But the country also has *zakat* and other Islamic taxes, together with a reputation for extraordinary corruption in tax administration, which discourages compliance even by honest taxpayers. Like the country in general, Pakistan is best described as a hybrid of British, Islamic, and Indian traditions, with the weight of each depending on the time, place, and the particular problem at issue.[40] Fitting the country into any single category is a difficult and perhaps an impossible task.

Post-revolutionary Iran is another example of a country whose tax system reflects disparate historical, geographic, and religious influences. The country has a nominally progressive income tax but with large sectors of the economy remaining effectively tax-exempt, a situation enabled to some degree by the country's oil receipts, which account for approximately half of government revenues. The country also makes numerous distinctions between domestic and foreign enterprises and features several free trade zones that provide tax and other incentives to foreign

38 See generally Assaf Likhovski, *Tax Law and Social Norms.*

39 See generally Azim A. Nanji, "Ethics and Taxation: The Perspective of the Islamic Tradition," *Journal of Religious Ethics*, 13 (1) (1985), 161–78.

40 See generally Anita M. Weiss, *Islamic Reassertion in Pakistan: The Application of Islamic Laws in a Modern State* (New York: Palgrave MacMillian, 2014).

investors. Islamic taxes are collected on (in theory) a voluntary basis, notwithstanding the Islamic philosophy of the government as a whole.[41]

The countries above are only the most prominent examples of a broader phenomenon. In each corner of the world, tax policy and procedure reflects a mixture of global and local concerns, and an equally uneasy mixture of tax and nontax considerations. Values, attitudes, and institutions interact in an uneasy and often combustible mix that makes generalizations difficult and sometimes even dangerous to make. That a country is smaller or poorer than the "big players" in the field does not make it any less proud of its traditions or any more willing to bend to outside pressures. This is at bottom simply another way of saying that tax is a political subject and cannot be reduced to a syllogism or other mathematical formula. It is a lesson easily forgotten, but that has a tendency to reassert itself with a vengeance when ignored.

The survey above likewise suggests the role of historical contingency, as identified by Steinmo and others, in determining tax culture. The tax cultures of India and Israel reflect not solely or even primarily the values and attitudes of their own citizens, but the historical circumstance of their history of British occupation and their uneasy emergence from it. Russian and Chinese tax culture similarly reflect the two countries' diverse experience with communism: rejected in the Russian case, officially continuing but in a very different, almost unrecognizable way in China. Even for countries which were not subject to foreign occupation, like the United States, tax culture is an amalgam of current attitudes, existing and inherited institutions, and historical quirks or circumstance. Indeed, if one were forced to rank the factors in determining tax culture, it is likely that institutions would rank first, historical contingencies second, and current attitudes last in importance in many cases. This too is a lesson already observed in the abstract, but it is interesting to observe it in a somewhat more detailed case study.

## 5.7 LAW AND RELIGION: A (VERY) SLIGHT DIGRESSION

The discussion of Islamic taxes brings to mind a broader point about the relationship between law and religion, of which taxes are an important part. Western legal thought has tended to glorify the separation of law and religion, which supposedly began in the Reformation era and contributed to the rise of modern, secular legal systems. In a famous article by Harold Berman, this separation was among the principal factors that distinguished Western from non-Western legal systems, and – in Berman's view – contributed to the superiority, or at least the more advanced character, of the former.[42] Other factors cited by Berman, including the superior professionalism of Western law, the pluralism of its existing legal

[41] At this writing US sanctions complicate the Iranian economic and (indirectly) legal systems.
[42] H. Berman, *Law and Revolution*.

institutions, and its supposedly greater capacity for substantive change, were closely related to these differences.[43]

There are at least two problems with Berman's argument. The first is that Western law is often not nearly so secular as we pretend. Principles like human rights, the equality of women, and the sanctity of the individual are not neutral in character, but proceed logically and historically from the Christian – or if one prefers, the Judeo-Christian – tradition. Indeed, some scholars refer to these values as "secularized Christianity," and not always in a disparaging sense. Certainly this is the perception of many observers in the non-Christian (and especially the Islamic) world; and it is difficult to say that they are wrong.

A second problem is that it is hard to see why the separation of law and religion, or (what is closely related) law and morality, is invariably a good thing. Most of us would agree that there are forms of tax evasion which, even if arguably legal, are immoral or unethical in practice. The very concepts of fairness and equality are essentially moral rather than legal concepts and have their roots in religious thought.

While tax policy might seem less religious in origin than (say) criminal or family law, it is not entirely immune from religious influence. Many liberal scholars have cited religious injunctions to help the poor and vulnerable as arguments in favor of a progressive, redistributive tax system. By contrast, conservatives have cited the biblical tithe as an argument for a flat-rate tax and a generally lower level of government involvement.[44] The above are Christian (or Judeo-Christian) arguments, but similar texts are available in other traditions. Even the work of those secular philosophers who are typically cited in tax debates, like John Rawls, often has a quasi-Christian character, and can be difficult to express in other cultures.[45]

The point here is not to impose a theocracy, but to recognize that much of what we take to be "neutral" or "secular" in tax policy is in fact profoundly value-laden, and the values in question are usually Western – and not infrequently religious – in origin. That these values are obscured by neutral-sounding language, or that they have been adopted by many non-Western actors, does not make this any less true. With the relative decline of Western power this is likely to become more obvious. It is an important point to remember in considering tax culture and its evolution in the next century.

## 5.8 REPRISE: AMERICA AS A FOREIGN TAX JURISDICTION

Having examined the tax cultures of various foreign jurisdictions, it may be productive to come full circle and think again about our own American tax

43 Ibid.

44 I discuss these and related arguments in a previous article. See Michael A. Livingston, "Public Reason, Private Virtue, and Political Philosophy: Religious Approaches to the Progressive Income Tax," *Journal of Law, Religion & State*, 2 (2013), 168.

45 John Rawls, *A Theory of Justice* (Cambridge: Belknap Press, 1971).

culture.[46] What would we notice if we arrived from another planet, or from one of the other countries studied in this chapter, and looked at the United States as a foreign tax jurisdiction? What factors that seem normal to us would appear unusual or strange to an outsider who was not already familiar with them? If we had to explain the American tax system to a group of foreign students or tax officials, where would we begin?

Some of the outstanding factors would relate to the legal system as a whole. For example, the United States has a federal system, so that some taxes (e.g., sales and use taxes) exist exclusively at the state level, and federal courts are frequently called upon to determine the scope and limitations of state as well as federal levies. The United States also has a strong tradition of judicial review – what critics sometimes refer to as judicial lawmaking – so that an unusual amount of tax law is made by the courts, particularly when, as in the tax shelter/tax avoidance area, the statute is vague or indeterminate. The definition of income, which has been shaped almost entirely by the courts, is an obvious example. American society is also rather litigious in nature, so that there is a relatively high volume of litigation and other tax controversies as compared to other countries. This reflects, in part, the attitudes of individual Americans, but also the relative vagueness of many tax statutes and the willingness of the courts to intervene.

Other characteristics are more tax-specific in nature. The United States has a strong tradition of antitax sentiment, especially at the federal level, although (as previously noted) it also has a relatively good record of tax compliance, at least when compared to some other countries. The federal government is unusually dependent on the income tax, in part because other sources of revenue are traditionally the province of the states. Tax legislation is heavily politicized, albeit with a strong tradition of nonpartisan institutions like the Joint Tax Committee and the Treasury Department Office of Tax Policy, although this tradition has become frayed in recent decades with the increasing polarization of political parties and political discourse in general. As compared to other countries, lawyers have a greater role in the making and implementation of tax policy, although this has been somewhat diminished in favor of economists and other professions. Tax also has a somewhat higher profile in American law schools than in other countries.

American tax policy is also unique with regard to international transactions. The United States makes an unusually broad assertion of its worldwide taxing jurisdiction, resulting partly from its large size and partly from its political traditions.[47] American law firms tend to be larger than those in other countries and tax tends to be a more self-contained discipline in American law schools, although accounting firms (many of which now hire a large number of lawyers) have to some degree poached on this territory in recent years. The tax graduate

46 A shorter version of this analysis is in Chapter 1. This longer version is presented here to reflect the insights derived from the intervening chapters.

47 This is changing with the trend toward a territorial tax system, as reflected in the 2017 tax act.

(LL.M.) program, although it exists in other places, is also largely an American phenomenon.

One difficulty in defining an American tax culture is that the American government, law firms, and law schools have to a large degree exported that culture, so that many things which appear "neutral" or "universal" in nature are in fact American, or at least Anglo-American, in origin.[48] This is especially true with regard to business taxation, where American ideas like capital gain, affiliated group, and so forth have filtered into other countries' tax systems. More broadly, the entire discourse of modern tax policy is saturated with Anglo-American terminology (equity, efficiency, administrability) although some of it – most notably the Haig-Simons definition of income, which was actually borrowed from a German, Georg von Schanz – was originally imported from continental Europe.[49] The same is true for tax planning, tax evasion, and many similar concepts. Even the American idea of the law firm – large, multidepartmental, and with offices in more than one domestic as well as foreign cities – has to a certain degree been exported to other countries. It may accordingly take a little bit of digging to determine which of these features is authentically universal and which are actually American in origin, only later spreading to other locations.

Yet many aspects of American tax culture have not spread to other countries, and in some areas – particularly when one moves from business to individual and nonincome taxes – the gap is actually growing. For example, the United States is one of the few developed countries that does not have a value added tax, and one of the few to give the judiciary so much lawmaking power. Antitax feeling, in the American sense, has no precise parallel in most countries. Tax education, particularly in law school, likewise remains something of an outlier.[50] This is not to say that the United States lacks influence or (pace Donald Trump) that it is necessarily in some kind of retreat. It is simply to say that globalization goes only so far, and both large and small countries retain many distinctive aspects that change slowly, if at all, with the passage of time. Culture may be good and it may be bad, but it is never neutral. America is no exception.

## 5.9 THE UPSHOT: ONE TAX CULTURE OR MANY

In Chapter 4 we considered the rise of a global tax culture having largely American, or American-influenced, norms. The Asian resurgence and the persistence of national differences suggest a different possibility: a world with several competing tax cultures rather than a single dominant, Western worldview. A commonplace in most discussions of law, this development has been obscured by the superficial

48 This phenomenon was discussed in Chapter 4.

49 See generally Nancy C. Staudt, "The Political Economy of Taxation: A Critical Review of a Classic," *Law & Society Review*, 30 (1966), 651.

50 See Chapter 3.

similarity of tax systems and, perhaps, by a sense of tax as a "technical" area that is somehow immune from cultural differences. Yet these assumptions are often inaccurate, and they will be increasingly difficult to maintain in a future, Asian-centered world. Even outside of Asia, the rise of countries (Brazil, Russia, South Africa) and regions (the Islamic world) that were previously marginalized in tax discourse suggests a major and potentially irreversible shift in direction, with non-Western or non-American views having increasing weight in tax matters. This change may be faster or slower, but it is bound to come.

The end of Western dominance affects not only the answers to tax questions, but sometimes the very questions themselves. Chinese tax policy emphasizes the collective rather than the individual impact of tax decisions and assumes a fundamentally different relationship between the state, its citizen, and its legal and administrative institutions. Islamic, and to some extent Indian, tax discourse sees taxes as one part of a larger religious or philosophical framework that is very different from Western assumptions. Words like "progressivity" or "redistribution," which have a positive connotation in Western Europe, are anathema only a few hundred miles to the east. Even within Western Europe there is a broad range of meanings: witness the difference between Nordic and American tax cultures, or between tax culture in northern Europe and the Mediterranean countries. To put things a little bit more poetically, the words of taxation may be the same everywhere, but the music is often different, both in an academic context and in the realm of day-to-day tax matters.

The shift in power calls into question the convergence of legal systems, which is historically the goal of comparative law.[51] It raises the specter that legal and tax cultures may not become more similar but may actually be drifting further apart. More ominously, it suggests that the very idea of "convergence" or globalization may itself be offensive, a thinly veiled rationalization for the maintenance of Western ideological and cultural supremacy that is now well past its sell-by date. Certainly it has been, and often continues to be, seen this way in the developing world. This is a problem for all areas of comparative law, but it is arguably a greater problem for fields like tax where convergence on major issues has been taken for granted, and the existence of different tax cultures has to some degree been ignored.

The discussion above has been conducted at a necessarily high level of generality. But comparative law works best at a detailed, microscopic level. How have the themes above expressed themselves in specific areas of tax law and practice, and how is this process different now than it was a generation ago? Are there some areas in which tax law is converging and others where the differences between countries are holding steady or even growing in nature? What, if anything – subject matter, history, ideology – distinguishes the first category from the second, and which, if either, category is likely to grow in the future? It is to this discussion that we now turn.

[51] See Chapter 1.

# 6

# Case Studies II: Progressivity, Tax Avoidance, and Environmental Taxes

To this point we have proceeded topically and (to a lesser extent) geographically, delineating the field of tax and culture and considering its application to various countries and political systems. But cultural differences matter only to the extent that they produce different outcomes with respect to the same or similar issues. This can be studied, in turn, only by choosing one or more specific tax problems and seeing how they are dealt with in different cultural environments. To put the matter more pithily, this is a work of comparative law, and it is time to make some comparisons; or (with apologies to Clifford Geertz) to proceed from thinner to thicker descriptions of the issues at hand.

I have chosen for this purpose three issues, two of which I have written about previously and the third of which I have largely avoided. The first is the question of tax progressivity, specifically the progressive income tax and its role in different tax systems. How progressive are national tax systems, and is the level of progressivity determined by attitudes, institutions, history, or some other factors? Is there global convergence in the real and/or nominal level of tax progressivity, or have countries continued to go largely their own way?

The second is the phenomenon of tax avoidance and how different tax systems have responded to it. This is closely related to the progressivity question, since a sufficiently high level of tax avoidance will eventually undermine a progressive rate structure, but it is to some degree an independent issue. How have individual countries responded to this problem, and (once again) has their response been determined by institutional, attitudinal, or other factors? To what degree have countries cooperated, or at least coordinated their approaches to this issue, and to what degree have they gone their own way?

Third, I consider a newer issue, the response to environmental pollution and global warming and the role which taxes have played in that response. Have environmental taxes been introduced in each country, or (to the extent they've done anything) have they preferred a regulatory or an enforcement approach? Does the answer depend on broader political issues or on the tax culture of the country involved? How, if at all, does the answer here differ from that for the first two issues I have mentioned?

The chapter concludes with a note on "vertical borrowing" (i.e., borrowing by states from international organizations) and some thoughts on one area, family taxation, which appears to have converged relatively little with the passage of time. What happens when tax law interacts with another area of law that reflects deeply held social and cultural values? What does the answer to this question tell us about the convergence process and its applicability to different areas of law?

The topical nature of this chapter means that there is an inevitable degree of overlap with previous materials, which were organized around anthropological and sociological themes. Readers are asked to forgive this repetition in the interest of more robust conclusions. I will do my best to tie the principal themes together in Chapter 7.

## 6.1 LEGAL TRANSPLANTS AND "CONTAMINATION" OF LAW: A (BRIEF) THEORETICAL BACKGROUND

Before proceeding further, a bit of theoretical background is appropriate. The starting point here is the concept of legal transplants, associated most closely with Alan Watson but developed further by other scholars. This concept is closely related to the ideas of globalization and convergence of law, but it has a more specific meaning that is especially relevant to the tax field.

As defined by Watson in 1974,[1] a legal transplant is the movement of a rule or a system of law from one country to another, a phenomenon that has also been referred to as imitation, acculturation, and other terms. The idea has its origins in the historical jurisprudence of Savigny and other scholars, and has vague associations with Darwinism in the natural and social sciences. As understood by Watson, legal transplants have been a principal if not the principal source of legal change in the West since the days of the Roman Empire.

The idea of legal transplants would seem uncontroversial, but it has attracted a surprising degree of acrimony, which began almost immediately upon the publication of Watson's book. Some of this had to do with Watson himself, a somewhat unconventional legal scholar, and some of it with issues in Roman legal history, but there was also controversy regarding the more general argument of the book. A principal criticism was that Watson exaggerated the ease with which legal rules could be transferred between cultures, and, if taken far enough, seemed to reject the idea that law was or should be a reflection of a society's underlying values, then as now a starting point for legal theory particularly in English-speaking countries. The analogy to organ transplants, which were being attempted with mixed results at the

[1] Alan Watson, *Legal Transplants: An Approach to Comparative Law* (Athens: University of Georgia Press, 1974).

time, was frequently employed in this discussion. More recently, Piergiuseppe Monateri and other scholars have addressed legal transplants in the context of the European Union, which has attempted to speed up the voluntary borrowing process by imposing the "best" available rule on countries whose legal systems contain less successful rules, a process with predictably mixed results.[2]

How do transplants operate in the tax field? This question is addressed by Jinyan Li, cited previously in Chapter 4, in her 2013 article "Tax Transplants and the Critical Role of Processes: A Case Study of China."[3] In her article, Li notes that the literature in the tax field tends to assume a "common core" of tax rules and may be insufficiently sensitive to the differences in lawmaking processes between different countries. In the case of China, these include differences in political and administrative procedures but also in underlying values such as hierarchy, compromise, and a different understanding of the "rule of law" than exists in most Western countries.[4] Such differences are particularly important when would-be transplants affect personal and social norms of behavior rather than exclusively technical issues. According to Li, transplants that have taken adequate account of these differences have been successful in a Chinese context, while those that have not done so have been less successful.

There is a subtle but significant difference between the transplant concept and the idea of legal convergence as described in Chapter 1. Countries might conceivably converge toward similar rules because they encounter similar problems without necessarily adopting rules or practices originating in other places. (Children raised in isolation still learn how to walk.) Some legal borrowing might be unconscious in nature, like a student who imitates a teacher without realizing that he is doing so. Yet it seems clear that conscious borrowing, either voluntary or under economic and political compulsion, constitutes a significant part of the lawmaking process. For the remainder of this chapter we will consider these concepts more or less together, keeping an eye open for the degree of compulsion as opposed to voluntariness in the borrowing process.

The theory of legal transplants is likewise related to, but distinct from, the network concept associated with David Singh Grewal and other scholars.[5] Like the network concept, it implies an ongoing process of communication and comparison, with the "best" rule eventually displacing less attractive alternatives. In this sense it resembles

2 *See* Pier Giuseppe Monateri, "The Weak Law: Contamination and Legal Cultures," *Transnational Law & Contemporary Problems*, 13 (2003), 575. An appreciation of Watson and his significance is Gary L. Francione, "Alan Watson: Some Reflections on a Great Legal Scholar and Teacher, and a Wonderful Friend," *Georgia Journal of International & Comparative Law*, 41 (3) (2013), 595–604. The Francione piece is part of a longer colloquium on Watson and his influence.

3 *Journal of Chinese Tax and Policy*, 3 (2013), 85.

4 These issues are discussed in Chapter 5.

5 David Singh Grewal, *Network Power: The Social Dynamics of Globalization* (New Haven: Yale Press, 2008).

Grewal's analogy of people agreeing to meet at the most likely location in a new city even without an explicit agreement to do so.[6]

But the term "transplant" implies a stronger resistance to this process in law than might be the case in (say) food, entertainment, telecommunications, or other nonlegal fields. The transplant theory is thus simultaneously older and more ambivalent than the globalization concept, dating to the era of the Roman Empire, but conscious of the difference between peoples and cultures and aware that resistance to "foreign" ideas may be especially potent in the legal arena because of its historical tie to national sovereignty and real or imagined national values. To turn Grewal's analogy on its head, a network must be especially potent in the legal arena, where people may come equipped with different frames of reference and may have strong incentives to disagree even on the appropriate place and time at which to begin their discussion. This does not mean that they will never reach agreement, but that the process of doing so may be longer, harder, and require more cultural sensitivity than would be the case in other areas of endeavor.[7]

## 6.2 CONTAMINATION AND GLOBALIZATION: OLD WINE IN NEW BOTTLES?

The transplant and contamination concepts are closely related to the newer and perhaps overused concept of the "globalization of law." As the name implies, the latter is essentially an extension of the theory of economic and political globalization to the legal field. The idea is that, as the nations of the world become more integrated in other ways, their legal systems will inevitably follow, so that we will someday no longer speak of American, Italian, or Chinese law but will instead speak of a single, unitary legal system. At this point, legal transplants would presumably be no longer an exception, but the norm: everybody's laws would be transplanted to and from everybody else's, so that the current geographic and cultural differences would become more or less insignificant. This is, of course, an overstatement: no one really believes that a unitary legal system exists now or is likely in the immediate future. But, as in other areas, the globalization concept provides a unifying theme, suggesting a direction that law might travel in even if it has not done so yet.

Globalization of law is an appealing concept, a comparativist's dream in which everyone adopts the correct rule and we all go home happy. The problem, of course, is that people raised in different legal cultures may find it difficult to agree on what the "correct" rule is. Even when they do agree, the agreement will frequently be superficial in nature, subject to interpretation and execution that makes similar-sounding rules have a very different practical effect. (That's what the last two

6 Ibid.

7 My real-life experience suggests that even Grewal's original example – a group of people agreeing to meet under the clock in New York's Grand Central Station – is more complex than he suggests. I would have assumed that we would meet at Times Square.

chapters were about.) Globalization of law thus runs the risk of being simultaneously too adventurous and not adventurous enough: too adventurous in that it underestimates the problem of agreement between legal cultures, and not adventurous enough in that it merely restates the phenomenon of legal transplants without the sophistication and historical awareness that attaches to the latter theory.

The issue of globalization of law has been addressed by the English legal philosopher William Twining, who has written on comparative law for several decades. Twining recognizes that there is indeed a globalization of law on a practical level, including increased attention to transnational legal issues, a resulting rethinking of domestic legal norms, and a growing interest in the diffusion of legal rules. But he is skeptical that a genuinely new theory of law has resulted from these developments, seeing most existing theories as essentially a reworking of traditional Western conceptions. In particular, he detects an excessive fascination with what he calls "surface law," that is, rules that appear similar to Western norms but are in fact applied quite differently in day-to-day life.[8] Twining suggests that before we can develop a truly global theory of law, we will need to gain further empirical understanding of the actual functioning of non-Western legal systems and their historic differences from traditional Western countries.

Somewhat more playfully, the French legal philosopher Jean-Bernard Auby uses the analogy of cooking (cuisine) as a metaphor for the accelerating but still incomplete globalization of legal norms.[9] According to Auby, globalization of law has advanced at both the vertical level (e.g., the European Union and other international organizations) and the horizontal level (i.e., the borrowing of norms between different national jurisdictions). But this process is inefficient both because different countries continue to have different values and because of the numerous imperfections in the borrowing process itself. This inefficiency results in a slow and uneven process of accommodation in which new global rules will continue to coexist with older, nationally based norms for the foreseeable future, with no clear resolution in sight.

Perhaps most cynical is the American scholar Bryant Garth, who describes what he calls "progressive legalization" as a reflection of imperial competition and hierarchies of power rather than a seamless process of convergence among equally powerful actors. Working together with the French scholar Yves Dezelay, Garth has produced a sociological theory of globalization that differs in many respects from the traditional narrative.[10] To a degree, Garth's analysis reflects the work of scholars outside the legal field who take a dim view of globalization as essentially the imposition of Western

8 See William Twining, *General Law: Understanding Law from a Global Perspective* (Cambridge University Press, 2012); cf. William Twining, *Globalisation and Legal Scholarship: Montesquieu Lecture* 2009 (Tilburg Law Lectures, Book Four) (Tilburg, Netherlands: Wolff Legal Publishers, 2011).

9 Jean-Bernard Auby, "Is Legal Globalization Regulated? Memling and the Business of Baking Camels," *Utrecht Law Review*, 4 (3) (2008), 210–17.

10 See, e.g., Y. Dezalay & B. Garth (eds.), *Lawyers and the Rule of Law in an Era of Globalization* (Abingdon-on-Thames: Routledge Press, 2011).

commercial culture on other, supposedly backward parts of the world. For example, George Ritzer, in his aptly titled "The Globalization of Nothing," paints a rather drab picture of globalization as the "McDonaldization" of daily human life, lacking in substance and devoid or even destructive of actual human feeling. [11] While not emphasizing law as a subject, Ritzer's work appears to be plainly pessimistic regarding the potential of globalization to adopt the "best" available practices in law any more than it has done in other substantive areas.

Scholars like Twining, Auby, and Garth cover a wide range of opinions, and it is difficult to summarize their views in a single paragraph. But it seems fair to say that all three are skeptical of the notion of globalization as an irreversible, all-encompassing process, and especially skeptical that the globalization of law will inevitably result in its improvement. This skepticism relates not only to the term globalization itself, but to the earlier concept of legal transplants and, indeed, to the basic concepts – that is, the functional approach and the "presumption of similarity" – that have dominated the field of comparative law for the better part of a century.[12]

By no means does this skepticism mean that traditional concepts are irrelevant or should be abandoned altogether. But it does suggest that they are likely to be uneven in application and to reflect existing power balances, both between and within countries, rather than constituting an unbiased search for the theoretically "best" rule in all available circumstances. Put in simpler terms, globalization of law shares the strengths and defects of globalization in general: a term that encompasses a wide variety of developments, useful for describing broad trends but best treated with some skepticism when applied to individual cases.

## 6.3 PROGRESSIVITY: ECONOMICS, CULTURE, AND THE QUESTION OF "TAX LIFE CYCLES"

We begin our discussion of borrowing and convergence with the question of tax rates and the overall design of income tax systems. With the exception of Eastern Europe, all or nearly all advanced countries have some form of progressive tax system on individual and (sometimes) business income. These include countries, like the United States and China, which would probably find few areas of agreement on other legal or cultural matters. To what extent did these systems develop independently of one another, to what extent did they develop together, and are they converging or diverging from one another?

A bit of background may be appropriate here. Progressive taxation refers to the imposition of higher rates on increasing levels of income, often referred to as tax or income brackets. (The United States presently has seven brackets for individual

[11] George Ritzer & Michael Ryan, "The Globalization of Nothing, in Postmodernism, Globalization and Politics," *Social Thought and Research*, 25 (1/2) (2002), 51–81.

[12] See Chapter 2.

income, ranging from 10 to 37 percent, eight if the implicit 0-percent tax rate on income below the first bracket is included.) In theory, this results in a higher-income taxpayer not only paying more tax than one with lower income, but paying tax at a higher marginal rate.

The arguments for progressivity are well-rehearsed, including the so-called marginal utility of income (each additional dollar of income is, in theory, less important to a rich person than a poor one), the potential injustice of the pretax distribution of income, and the benefit theory, which states that the wealthy benefit from government services more than the poor.[13] Against this are arrayed various arguments emphasizing the individual's right to keep her own income, the potentially damaging effects of progressive taxation on the work ethic, and so forth. These arguments are more or less universal in nature, although of course their persuasiveness varies with time, place, and the person you happen to be talking to. As a general rule progressivity has been on the defensive in recent years,[14] a combination of theoretical trends and various tax avoidance strategies, but it retains a stubborn if (in the words of a famous article) uneasy hold on the popular imagination and is unlikely to disappear any time soon.

In a previous series of articles I discussed the issue of progressive taxation in four countries: the United States, Italy, Israel, and India.[15] I found that each of these countries maintained progressive income tax systems, but there were substantial differences between the situation in each country and, sometimes, between an individual country's reality and popular perceptions of it. For example, the United States – notwithstanding its frequently conservative image – maintained a relatively high level of progressivity, although this had come under increasing challenge in recent years, and although effective tax rates (that is, after considering the effect of deductions, credits, etc.) were lower than stated or nominal rates. By contrast, Italy and Israel, although philosophically further left than the United States, appeared to have rather leaky tax systems, especially where capital income was concerned: when all these factors were taken into account it was difficult to say whether these countries actually had a more progressive tax system than the United States. By contrast, China and India were in many respects outliers: they maintained progressive tax systems on paper, but their tax brackets were set up in such a way that only

13 These and other arguments are collected in Walter J. Blum & Harry Kalven, Jr., "The Uneasy Case for Progressive Taxation," *University of Chicago Law Review*, 19 (1952), 417.

14 The past decade shows some signs of a reversal of this trend, especially in the United States, but it is hard to tell if this is a temporary or a permanent change.

15 Michael A. Livingston, "Blum and Kalven at 50: Progressive Taxation, Globalization, and the New Millenium," *Florida Tax Review*, 11 (2000), 731; Michael A. Livingston, "From Milan to Mumbai Changing in Tel Aviv: Reflections on Progressive Taxation and 'Progressive' Politics in a Globalized But Still Local World," *American Journal of Comparative Law*, 54 (3) (2006), 555–74; Michael A. Livingston, "From Mumbai to Shanghai with a Side Trip to Washington: China, India and the Future of Progressive Taxation in an Asian-Led World," *Theoretical Inquiries in Law*, 11 (2010), 539. It was largely coincidence that the first three countries began with an "I" – I have never been to Iraq or Iran, and only once to Iowa, although I have since visited Iceland.

a relatively small part of the population paid the income tax at all. (This situation is changing as more people earn higher incomes, somewhat more rapidly in the Chinese than the Indian case.) In these countries, progressive income taxation was arguably more symbolic than substantive in nature – like a country having a steel plant, aircraft carrier, or its own national flag airline – with the real work of revenue-raising being done elsewhere in the system, particularly by the VAT and other excise taxes, and most income redistribution being accomplished by spending rather than tax provisions.

Even more interesting than the differences described above were the reasons they existed. Contrary to my expectations, I found that institutions were usually more important than attitudes in determining each country's experience with progressive taxation and taxation in general. Thus, American federalism, separation of powers, and the role of lawyers as well as economists in tax policy seemed at least as important in determining outcomes as the country's supposed individualism or reputed aversion to redistributive policies. Italy's position in the EU, and Israel's emphasis on redistribution through spending rather than tax measures, were equally or more significant than the former's alleged hostility to authority or the latter's socialist tradition. China seemed less influenced by Marxist ideology than by the conflict between a growing need for revenue and the public's limited experience with tax filing and tax administration. Indian taxation was influenced by its colonial history and the country's federal structure as much as or more than longstanding Hindu traditions or the more recent Gandhian reforms. Indeed, it was this surprising dominance of institutional factors, and the corresponding gap between attitudes and outcomes in one country after another that I studied, that led me to embark on the instant "tax and culture" project.

Perhaps the most interesting finding was the role of historical quirks or accidents in each of the countries studied. Progressivity in India was hampered by the national (Union) government's historic inability to tax agricultural income, a colonial holdover that no one seemed able to state a coherent policy reason for. Italy kept its capital gain rate low in part because it believed that a higher rate would cause Milan investors, who accounted for about half the country's capital gains, to cross the nearby border to Switzerland. Israel had a long tradition of ignoring or incompletely taxing overseas income, which (like the agricultural rule in India) dated back to prestate times but had proved stubbornly difficult to overcome.[16] Much of American antitax sentiment turned out to be directed at spending rather than taxes: state and local taxes, which were more regressive and sometimes higher than federal ones, attracted significantly less opposition. (It may also be that people were simply less aware of them.) Any one of these factors could be dismissed as a mere aberration, but in the aggregate they made it difficult for each of the countries to achieve a rational,

[16] These issues were discussed in prior chapters.

progressive tax system: in a sense, they *were* the system in each country, and tax officials had little choice but to work around them in making policy choices.

Scandinavia, which I studied after these articles came out, was similarly quirky: it had high tax rates but not especially progressive ones, and its tax culture was tied to a level of social spending and perhaps homogeneity that was hard to duplicate elsewhere.[17] Indeed, the Nordic countries were diverging from one another, with Norway increasingly reliant on oil revenues (another geographic quirk) and Denmark somewhat more insistent than Sweden on maintaining its high tax, high spending model. All three countries struggled with unprecedented immigration and its possible deleterious effect on the Nordic Model. Here again, institutions seemed to have been more important than popular attitudes, and unique or random elements – what I charitably termed "historical factors" – arguably most important of all. There appears to be little reason to think that other countries or regions would differ from this pattern.

Are the countries studied converging with respect to tax progressivity? Yes and no. Following the 1980s US tax reform, the countries of Isreal, India, and Italy had reduced their top marginal tax rates and made at least some effort to increase their tax base, at least formally following the American model. (Even Sweden had a US-style tax reform in the 1990s, although retaining its essential welfare state more or less intact.) But base-broadening in all these countries failed to achieve its promise, and rate reduction was highly uneven, depending on the country in question, the type of income, and numerous other factors. In this as in other areas, formal convergence was more convincing than the substantive kind: tax systems "on the ground" remained markedly different from one another, a reality that showed no obvious signs of changing anytime soon. This was especially true when real tax rates, taking into account both legal deductions/exclusions and illegal or quasilegal tax forms of tax evasion, were taken into account rather than the nominal variety.

A major reason for the failure of convergence was the persistence of institutional factors and historical quirks, which proved resistant to a leveling tendency even where popular attitudes were not especially different in the countries concerned. Indeed, these factors sometimes appeared to be pulling countries further apart rather than pushing them closer together. This was especially noticeable in the Nordic region, where Sweden and Denmark followed increasingly different paths, and Norway, awash with oil revenues, faced a radically different set of choices. At times, centrifugal forces operated even within countries: antitax sentiment remained strong in the "red" American states (primarily in the south and west) while the "blue" states, most notably California, enacted tax increases. Political movements like Trumpism in the United States, Brexit in the United Kingdom, or the Five Star Movement in Italy suggested a powerful reaction against political, economic, and legal convergence that showed no signs of abating anytime soon.

[17] Steinmo's analysis of Swedish tax policy is discussed in Chapter 3.

One interesting question in studying progressive taxation was that of tax history or what might be called "tax life cycles." There appears to a pattern in which countries that reach a certain state of economic development – the UK in the nineteenth century, the United States in the early twentieth century, China and India today – feel the need for an income tax both as an improved source of revenue and to break up new and unprecedented concentrations of income. As more people have higher incomes – and as the need for revenue grows – the tax covers more and more people, but eventually it hits diminishing returns, and resistance to the tax grows along with increasingly creative and aggressive forms of tax evasion. At some point, still in the future, the most advanced countries will either give up on the tax altogether or allow so many exclusions and deductions that the income tax becomes effectively a tax on labor income with the capital portion of the tax (somewhat like the US estate tax) more or less elective in nature. This argument suggests less a borrowing process than a natural course of events that countries follow independently but that leads them to more or less the same place.

Neither the role of historical quirks nor the (highly debatable) theory of tax life cycles means that the convergence process is insignificant or that it will not win out in the long run. Phenomena that seem permanent or inevitable in one era sometimes prove ephemeral in another. (How's that "end of history" thing been working out for you, Professor Fukuyama?) But the long run, as Keynes reminded us, is a very long time, and opposing forces are likely to remain powerful for the foreseeable future. As Oscar Wilde might have said, I can predict anything except the future.

## 6.4 TAX AVOIDANCE: THE LIMITS OF CONVERGENCE AND THE ROLE OF TAX TRANSPLANTS

Closely related to the issue of progressive taxation is the question of tax avoidance. High tax rates accomplish little if income is simply exempted, hidden, or else shifted to a lower-tax jurisdiction. (This phenomenon has been colorfully referred to as "digging deeply with a sieve.")[18] The war against tax avoidance, and the boundary between legitimate and illegitimate efforts at tax reduction, accordingly constitute a central part of tax administration in every country. As money moves more and more easily across international boundaries, it might even be said that the war against tax avoidance is the starting point for the entire discussion of the progressivity issue.

A bit of background may be useful here. It is generally accepted that taxpayers have the right to engage in tax reduction or what is somewhat euphemistically called "tax planning." However, tax avoidance or (more heinously) tax evasion is typically proscribed. Where the line between these concepts lies is frequently difficult to determine. Perhaps the most famous case on this subject, the US Supreme Court's

[18] The phrase is often attributed to Henry Simons, although I am not sure it has been verified.

decision in *Gregory* v. *Helvering*,[19] states that a transaction should have a legitimate "business purpose" – that is, a purpose other than the reduction of taxes – in order to be respected for tax purposes. But business purpose is a notoriously slippery concept, often resulting in long and arduous litigation, and has been difficult to apply with any reasonable degree of consistency. In any case, the concept applies only in the United States and others who have followed its example; it is by no means universal in nature.

The war against tax evasion is difficult enough within one country but becomes exponentially more difficult when cross-border transactions are involved. This is true for several related reasons. First, money moves easily over national borders, and it tends to seek out the most favorable tax treatment – the tax arbitrage phenomenon discussed in Chapter 4. The international tax system is thus, in a very literal sense, only as strong as its weakest link. Indeed, it can at times be difficult even to gather information about money or assets in a foreign country, especially in so-called tax haven jurisdictions that are chosen for their opaque character and have little, if any, incentive to be more transparent. Efforts to compel the provision of financial information, like the American FACTA legislation,[20] have been only partially successful and generated substantial resentment. A recent book the French economist Gabriel Zucman suggests that the tax haven phenomenon is significantly larger than generally suspected and is getting worse with time.[21]

Together with these practical problems there are important issues of tax culture. What constitutes illegal tax evasion as opposed to permissible tax reduction is a question that varies significantly between countries and sometimes within the same country. The question is not merely a tax matter, but a matter of legal and moral principles as well as taxpayer attitudes: as observed in Chapter 5, it can be difficult to prevent tax avoidance when people do not accept the underlying validity of the existing tax system itself. The responsibility for combating tax evasion may likewise be allocated differently, with the tax administration having primary responsibility for combatting tax evasion in some countries and the courts or the legislature taking a more important role in others.

Finally, considerations of national pride and self-interest may outweigh the urge to cooperate in fighting tax evasion, especially when the countries requesting such cooperation, like Germany and France in the EU or the United States throughout the western hemisphere, are perceived as imperious or overbearing in nature. (The current problems of the EU result, in part, from precisely this sort of feeling.) At the very least, smaller and poorer countries may demand compensation, monetary or otherwise, in return for cooperating. Even one country failing to do so may be sufficient to undermine certain schemes.[22]

19 293 U.S.465 (1935).

20 Foreign Account Tax Compliance Act, Pub. L. 111–47 (2010).

21 Gabriel Zucman, *The Hidden Wealth of Nations: The Scourge of Tax Havens* (Chicago: University of Chicago Press, 2015).

22 The BEPS Project, described in Chapter 4, is an example of this phenomenon.

Perhaps the most sophisticated study of comparative tax avoidance has been conducted by Assaf Likhovski. In a series of books and articles Likhovski examines the response to tax avoidance in Israel, the United States, the United Kingdom, and other countries, including both specific judicial decisions and broader administrative approaches. This research is part of his more comprehensive study of cultural factors in tax decision-making and the role of tax transplants, which Likhovski finds frequently take on a new and unrecognizable form when they arrive in a different host country. (The effort to import British tax concepts to the Middle East region, and its inevitable limitations, is one of many interesting examples of this adaptive process.)[23]

One of Likhovski's principal findings – and a recurring theme of research in comparative tax law generally – is the difficulty in separating tax-specific decisions from their broader legal, political, and institutional context. For example, while British judges have historically taken a rather formalist approach to tax evasion, the United States Supreme Court adopted a more forceful "business purpose" approach – effectively adding a judicial gloss to the underlying statute – in the famous *Gregory* case,[24] a decision which Likhovski attributes to a mixture of doctrinal and political considerations, including concerns about the morality of tax avoidance and contemporary newspaper reports regarding aggressive tax avoidance by wealthy, politically prominent individuals.[25] The difference in outcomes, Likhovski implies, resulted not so much from different tax circumstances as different understandings of the courts and their appropriate institutional role.

By contrast, the early Israeli courts, although the country had legislated a statutory antiavoidance provision, were reluctant to employ that provision and adopted a more limited form-and-substance approach, an outcome which Likhovski attributes primarily to concerns regarding the limitations of the young nation's tax enforcement capacity.[26] These historical and institutional factors led to different outcomes from those in the United Kingdom or the United States – older countries and more secure in their tax administration ability – although all three countries presumably opposed tax avoidance and the issues that they faced were substantively rather similar in nature. Had the same judges decided these cases in a different country or historical context, Likhovski's research implies, the results might well have been the opposite in each of the three cases studied.

[23] See Assaf Likhovski, *Tax Law and Social Norms in Mandatory Palestine and Israel* (Cambridge University Press, 2017).

[24] 293 U.S.365 (1935).

[25] Assaf Likhovski, "The Duke and the Lady: Gregory v. Helvering and the History of Tax Avoidance Adjudication," *Cardozo Law Review*, 25 (2004), 953. *Gregory* involved the use of a tax-free reorganization to effect the distribution and subsequent sale of shares at a substantially reduced tax rate. The statute said nothing about the purpose of the transaction.

[26] Assaf Likhovski, "Formalism and Israeli Anti-Avoidance Doctrines in the 1950s and 1960s, in Studies" in John Tiley (ed.), *History of Tax Law* (Oxford: Hart Publishing, 2004).

Likhovski's work suggests the pattern of superficial convergence and underlying difference that lies at the heart of tax culture. While all countries oppose tax avoidance, in practice their approaches are quite different and depend on a variety of factors including the economic and political situation, the aggressiveness of tax administrators, and the broader legal system. Historical factors like the tradition of judicial review in the United States, the formalist impulse in the United Kingdom, or the limited capacity of the Israeli state may be more important than specifically tax doctrines or the facts of individual cases. This is even before one reaches "national security" and other political factors that may relegate tax policy to a low rung on the priority scale. None of this would surprise comparative law scholars but it is easy to ignore in the tax field, with its unstated assumption that all countries face essentially similar issues and will eventually confront them in more or less similar ways. As the saying goes, "the devil is in the details," and where tax law is concerned it is often the details that matter most.[27] It's an old lesson but easily forgotten.

## 6.5 TAX MEETS GLOBAL WARMING: THE PROBLEM OF ENVIRONMENTAL TAXES

Progressive taxation and its cousin, tax avoidance, have been around for a long time. A more recent challenge involves technological change and its accumulating effect on the human environment, an effect that some believe may prove fatal to human life if it is not counteracted.[28] Taxes are often, although not always, one of the alternatives for dealing with this problem. How have tax systems responded to this newer development, and how has this response differed in different places and at different times? What, if anything, do the answers tell us about the problem of tax culture and the tax transplant question?

Before proceeding to this question, a bit of history is useful. Tax professionals tend to think that the purpose of taxation is raising revenue and anything beyond that is somebody else's problem. But taxes have frequently been used to encourage desired behavior and discourage unwanted activities. Tax incentives, or disincentives, are especially attractive when they raise revenue at the same time that they impact individual behavior: cigarette and alcohol taxes are an obvious case in point, although the revenue that they produce may (ironically) be reduced if they succeed in decreasing consumption. In this sense, environmental taxes are simply a modern and more extensive version of what is historically an old problem.

Pollution, as it was called in gentler times, is an especially attractive territory for this brand of tax engineering. From an economist's perspective, pollution is an

27 Both this statement and the offsetting "God is in the details" have been attributed to several people; Bartlett's Quotations lists it as anonymous.

28 See, e.g., Union of Concerned Scientists, "Global Warming Impacts: The consequences of climate change are already here," (October 8, 2019) www.ucsusa.org/our-work/global-warming/science-and-impacts/global-warming-impacts.

"externalities" problem: the polluter reaps the benefits of her economic activity but is not required to bear the associated economic or social costs. Put more bluntly, the polluter gets the benefit while the rest of society pays the price.

The obvious solution is to make her share the costs by means of a tax or similar payment, a solution that is sometimes referred to as a Pigovian tax after the Cambridge economist, Arthur C. Pigou, who developed the concept.[29] The revenues from such taxes could also be used, in theory, to fund renewable energy sources and other alternatives to fossil fuels, thereby reducing pollution while increasing alternate energy supplies or (less optimally) to clean up the resulting pollution. Taxes are hardly the only strategy for dealing with this problem: so-called cap and trade programs, nontax incentives, and direct government regulation also come to mind, and may be preferable if one believes that global warming is an immediate and potentially irreversible threat to human survival. (Taxes tend to provide incremental rather than radical solutions, and they often work rather slowly.) But they are one obvious approach and may be less onerous than the available alternatives, or involve fewer administrative costs.

If the arguments in favor of environmental taxes are predictable then so are the arguments against them. Such taxes, it is said, will impose large economic cost and have only a marginal effect on global warming and similar environmental problems. They will be highly regressive in nature, hitting the middle class and poorer consumers most heavily, and they will contribute to larger government and less private initiative. Even if the taxes should prove successful in one country, the polluters will simply take their business elsewhere, leaving the overall environment unchanged but transferring economic growth and prosperity away from the countries or regions that impose environmental taxes and toward the places that do not.[30] To some extent these are generic antitax arguments, but they are reinforced by doubts (or professed doubts) about the extent of global warming and related environmental crises.

The suggestion that a carbon tax will cause polluters to move elsewhere, thus failing to reduce the aggregate volume of pollution, is especially interesting. Obviously, this takes place to some degree. But what if environmental problems cause people rather than businesses to move away? An argument to this effect, known as displacement theory, has become popular in environmental circles. Indeed, the argument suggests that environmentally generated movements of population may be the next great human rights issue, as people from (say) Bangladesh flee the flooding of coastal lowlands, or those in Latin America the destruction of rain forests, and so forth. (Bangladesh has over 165 million people, most of them with relatively low incomes.) This argument might suggest that, in the long run, discouraging pollution by taxes or other measures might actually be a good investment

29 Arthur C. Pigou, *The Economics of Welfare* (London: Macmillan and Co., 1920).

30 The arguments for and against environmental taxes are summarized by John Wihbey, "Pros and Cons of a Carbon Tax: Key Issues" (July 20, 2016), www.yaleclimateconnections.org/2016/07/pros-and-cons-of-a-carbon-tax-key-issues/.

for the country in question. On the other hand, if a tax merely causes polluters to move from high-tax to low-tax jurisdictions, or from high-income to lower-income areas, each of which have less ability to combat the resulting pollution, it could make the situation worse. Displacement theory also has little to say about the effectiveness of tax as opposed to nontax measures: it is primarily an argument about effects rather cause.

Reuven Avi-Yonah and David Uhlmann have argued that a carbon tax is indeed a superior approach to a cap and trade program or other regulatory approaches.[31] Among the arguments they advance are the simplicity of a tax system, its revenue impact, and its ability to "signal" a proenvironment policy more effectively than other methods. These arguments are largely similar to the arguments for tax deductions and credits that have appeared in other circumstances, including housing policy and credits for alternative energy courses.[32] The authors concede various limitations to their proposal, including political resistance and the likelihood of politically inspired exemptions for selected users, but believe these arguments are outweighed by the advantages above.[33] Similar arguments have been advanced by other scholars, although there have also been some criticisms.

Given the political nature of these arguments – and of environmental issues in general – there is, not surprisingly, a substantial divergence in environmental tax policy, with some countries rushing to enact such taxes and so far a larger number resisting them. Also not surprisingly, there is a strong correlation between environmental tax policy and a nation's overall approach to both environmental and tax issues. As predicted by Avi-Yonah and Uhlmann, the taxes that have been enacted were political compromises, involving significant exemptions and concessions for politically connected producers and users. This is in addition to many countries whose preexisting tax policies – income tax, VAT, sales and use taxes – impose an indirect cost on energy consumption or, in some cases, seek actively to encourage it.

Probably the best example of an explicit tax on energy consumption is Sweden. The Swedish carbon tax (*koldioxidskatt*), in effect since 1991, imposes a charge of about $150 per ton of carbon dioxide, which comes to something like an additional dollar per gallon of gasoline and an equivalent amount on other uses. There is an exemption for fuels from renewable sources and fuels used to produce electricity, which (like other energy sources) is subject to a separate tax. (This in addition to Sweden's already high income, VAT, and other taxes.) Industrial as opposed to

31 Under a cap and trade system, countries or localities are given pollution "credits" which they can then trade with other entities: the idea is to permit a degree of flexibility while holding the overall volume of pollution constant. The European Union currently has such a system in place under the name of ETS (Emissions Trading System); the Obama administration attempted but failed to enact one.

32 Edward Zelinsky, "Efficiency and Income Taxes: The Rehabilitation of Tax Incentives," *Texas Law Review*, 64 (1986), 973.

33 Reuven S. Avi-Yonah & David M. Uhlmann, "Combating Global Climate Change: Why a Carbon Tax Is a Better Response to Global Warming than Cap and Trade," *Stanford Environmental Law Journal*, 28 (2009), 3.

residential users pay the tax at a 50-percent rate, a concession which has blunted somewhat the political opposition to the tax.[34]

The carbon tax has been credited with a significant reduction in carbon emissions – the Swedish government claims a 25-percent reduction while GNP has increased by more than half – although it has also been criticized (perhaps inevitably) for being both too aggressive and not aggressive enough. As is typical of Sweden's consensus-style politics, the tax appears to have garnered support so far from all but fringe political parties: the principal debates appear to concern the amount of the tax and the nature of the exemptions rather than its existence.[35] The tax is one part of a broader environmental policy including green buses, a general emphasis on mass transit, and (more recently) a proposed tax on airport departures, designed to raise revenue but also to discourage unnecessary air travel, which the long distances in Scandinavia have made increasingly popular.[36]

The Swedish example has been followed to varying degrees in the remaining Nordic countries, with Denmark, Norway, and Finland all enacting some form of carbon tax – generally less extensive than the Swedish model – together with various nontax initiatives to reduce carbon consumption and encourage alternative fuels. This is consistent with the general pattern in the region, under which progressive tax policies are combined with an environmentally conscious approach at both a public and private level.[37] The relative insulation of energy policy from political cycles, with most major parties agreeing on the priority of environmental issues if inevitably disagreeing on certain details, has also played a role.

Norway presents an especially interesting case. Understandably wishing to preserve its spectacular natural environment, the country has become a world leader in electric cars and other sustainable technology, policies which are frequently touted in the nation's self-promotion efforts. But Norway is also a substantial oil producer, primarily from offshore wells located in the North Sea, and the great majority of this oil is exported to foreign countries. This has led to predictable criticism that the country is attempting to reduce its own carbon footprint at the expense of other, less privileged locations, effectively exporting pollution to the outside (and primarily less developed) world. That Norway has a per capita GNP in excess of $70,000 per year – only Luxembourg, Switzerland, and by some measures Macau rank higher

34 See generally www.carbontax.org/where-carbon-is-taxed/#Sweden (September 10, 2017).

35 The Sweden Democrats, on the right wing of Swedish politics, garnered about 17 percent of the vote in the most recent national elections but were effectively excluded from the negotiations on formation of a new government: whether or how long this situation will last is unclear.

36 Among other policies, there are fees for driving into central Stockholm, an office block which uses body heat to stay warm, and (I promise I'm not making this up) buses that run on energy from the entrails of slaughtered cows. See Gwladys Fouché, "Sweden's Carbon-Tax Solution to Carbon Change Puts It Top of the Green List," *The Guardian* (April 28, 2008). At this writing the airport tax is still at the proposal stage. The somewhat theatrical "school strike for the climate," led by 16-year-old Greta Thunberg, has increased the political pressure for stricter environmental measures in Sweden and other countries.

37 See the discussion of Nordic tax policy in Chapter 5.

according to the most recent statistics – makes this accusation especially politically sensitive.

The Norwegian government has responded to these challenges by undertaking various ameliorative policies, including purchasing carbon credits, investing in overseas rainforests, and providing assistance in "sustainability" strategies to other oil-producing countries. These are politically attractive compromises but have led to inevitable charges of hypocrisy by environmental activists.[38] At least one challenge has been somewhat more dramatic, with the environmental group Greenpeace taking the government to court in an effort to block new drilling in the Barents Sea. While proving unsuccessful at the trial court level, the case is at this writing on appeal to the Norwegian Supreme Court.[39] Most Norwegian political parties appear to accept the government's current policy, albeit with varying degrees of enthusiasm: the use of oil revenues to support the country's generous welfare state is one reason.

The record in the rest of Europe is somewhat mixed, the results depending in part on definition. For example, the United Kingdom maintains an effective carbon tax ("carbon price floor"), although this does not show up in tax revenues.[40] France attempted to impose a carbon tax on top of already existing fuel taxes, and was rewarded by a truck drivers' strike (the so-called *gilet jaune* movement) that resulted in large-scale violence and eventually led to the proposal's withdrawal. (In fairness, there were other issues at stake in the strike, including the unpopularity of the French President and general social unrest as well.) The EU has a goal of environmental taxes reaching 10 percent of aggregate revenues by 2020, although most countries have yet to reach this threshold.

In addition to France, Italy has proposed subsidies on ecological (primarily electric) cars to be financed by a tax on polluting vehicles, although the tax – which has been subject to similar if less radical criticisms than the French version – has yet to be enacted. Britain has a more limited tax on coal used to produce electricity and is considering a broader tax if a "no-deal Brexit" should take it out of the more general European price floor. Australia, Ireland, Chile, and a number of other countries have also experimented with various forms of direct or indirect carbon taxes.

Closer to home, four Canadian provinces – British Columbia, Quebec, and (more recently) Alberta, and Ontario – impose carbon taxes of various forms, and Prime Minister Justin Trudeau has announced a plan under which the remaining

38 See, e.g., www.seattletimes.com/nation-world/paradox-nation-norway-a-climate-leader-making-money-on-oil/ (July 31, 2016).

39 See Megan Darby, "Greenpeace Appeals Norway Arctic Oil Drilling Case" (May 2, 2018), www.climatechangenews.com/2018/02/05/greenpeace-appeal-norway-arctic-oil-drilling-case/.

40 See generally www.carbontax.org/where-carbon-is-taxed/ (September 10, 2017). Australia repealed its existing carbon tax in 2014. Germany, France, and other European countries participate in a carbon trading system and similar measures but do not yet have a full-blown carbon tax.

provinces would be required to introduce either a similar tax or an alternative cap and trade system beginning in 2018.[41] The goal would be a minimum cost of CAN$10 per ton of emissions in 2018, rising to CAN$50 per ton in 2022. The proposal has led to some controversy, notably regarding the exemptions provided to particular uses in the existing provincial taxes, and whether the same exemptions will be extended to the national plan. (Environmental taxes are notorious for large, often politically inspired, exemptions for specific industries or uses.) While liberals support the proposals, conservatives have been skeptical, one opposing columnist suggesting that the tax was being disguised as an environmental measure and is really "all just clever spin to hide massive tax increases to fund big government."[42]

The United States has as yet no carbon tax, although one could argue that federal and state gasoline taxes have a parallel, if somewhat less comprehensive, effect.[43] Neither do Russia, China, or most other large countries. (Russia is also a very substantial, if sometimes unnoticed, energy exporter.) Voters in the state of Washington rejected an initial $15 per ton carbon tax following an at times surprising political debate, in which some energy producers supported the tax and many environmentalists actively opposed it, citing its regressive nature and its alleged failure to invest sufficient funds in clean energy alternatives.[44] (The proposal got approximately 40 percent of the vote.) Similar proposals have been made in other states.

At the national level, President Clinton proposed a so-called BTU (British thermal unit) tax that had many features similar to a carbon tax in the 1990s, but the proposal encountered strong opposition and was never enacted. Several members of Congress, including at least one Republican, have more recently introduced bills to impose a national carbon tax, although the fate of these proposals, together with other environmental legislation, remains uncertain at this writing.

The Washington vote is interesting because it suggests the complex nature of carbon tax politics, which depends on local conditions as well as timing concerns and can be difficult to place on a traditional conservative-liberal ("red-blue") axis. Perhaps because of this complexity, the divergence in environmental tax policy both between and within individual countries remains wide and is arguably even expanding in scope. The issue is

41 In 2019, the Canadian government took steps to impose a carbon tax on the four remaining provinces (Manitoba, New Brunswick, Ontario, and Saskatchewan) that had no such taxes of their own. Two additional provinces imposed such taxes in the interim.

42 See Candace Malcom, "Get Ready for Trudeau's Carbon Tax on Everything," *Toronto Sun* (May 19, 2017), www.torontosun.com/2017/05/19/get-ready-for-trudeaus-carbon-tax-on-everything.

43 Carbon taxes are more systematic than ordinary gasoline taxes in that they are imposed on all uses of carbon-based energy, subject to legislative exceptions, rather than selected uses. Gasoline taxes are frequently used to pay for further construction of highways and similar infrastructure that in the long run may aggravate environmental problems. See Internal Revenue Code sec. 9503 (creating the Highway Trust Fund).

44 See Chelsea Harvey, "It Could Be the Nation's First Carbon Tax, and Environmentalists Are Fighting over It," *Washington Post* (October 17, 2016), www.washingtonpost.com/news/energy-environment/wp/2016/10/17/it-could-be-the-nations-first-carbon-tax-and-environmentalists-are-fighting-over-it/.

also tied to broader political trends and sometimes to personal emotions. For example, the Trump administration's strong hostility toward energy taxes may actually have increased state interest in them, particularly in liberal or "blue" regions of the country, while liberal elites' support for carbon taxes in Europe may actually have made them even less palatable to conservative elements, who resent the liberals themselves as much as the taxes. The riots in France, which resulted in part from the imposition of carbon taxes but also from more general dissatisfaction with the Macron government and its alleged hauteur, are a particular case in point.

Does the divergence in carbon tax policy result primarily from environmental or tax issues? It can be difficult to say, since the same countries that are liberal on environmental policy are frequently liberal on taxes and vice-versa. But the arguments against environmental taxation (big government, decreased economic growth, loss of business to less scrupulous foreign competitors) sound an awful lot like the traditional arguments against tax increases generally. Many of the favorable arguments (incentives for good behavior, disincentives for bad, increased revenues for advantageous expenditures) are likewise similar to those made in other areas, and indeed are frequently made by the same people, who may have a variety of different motivations. While at times these arguments are connected to specifically environmental concerns, this is not always the case.

The faith or lack thereof that a country places in its tax institutions may likewise impact upon the choice between tax and nontax methods. Thus, even American liberals have tended to favor a market-based, cap and trade as opposed to a tax approach, while countries that place more faith in their tax systems (e.g., Sweden) are more likely to use environmental taxes. Conversely, some American conservatives have actually favored a tax approach, which they regard as at least being a market-oriented solution in contrast to a more direct spending or regulatory approach. In this respect, environmental taxes are as much a reflection of each country's tax culture as its environmental or energy philosophy.

The so-called yellow vest (*gilets jaunes*) riots in France provide an interesting case in point. The riots ostensibly resulted from the Macron government's proposal to increase environmental (i.e., fuel) taxes in order to meet the country's commitments under international agreements. Yet it quickly became apparent that the protesters had many grievances beyond tax policy – the high cost of living, resentment of urban elites, and (some alleged) antisemitic and anti-immigrant sentiment. The riots also took place against a background of the extreme unpopularity of President Macron and a high level of political confrontation in general. Finally, the taxes themselves were imposed in a regressive fashion on top of several other regressive taxes already in existence.[45] None of this means that environmental taxes will be popular in other

[45] Macron eventually withdrew his main proposal, but this did not end the protest movement. See Adam Nossiter, "France Suspends Fuel Tax Increase That Provoked Violent Protests," *N. Y. Times* (December 4, 2018), www.nytimes.com.

countries, or that there is an easy way to avoid the clash between environmental and tax policies. But it does suggest that a simplistic equation, under which environmental taxes are inherently popular with elites and unpopular with everyone else, may well be misleading: the actual result depends upon a mix of political, economic, and cultural factors that varies significantly between time and place.

This overlap between tax and nontax policy, and plain old political gamesmanship, is not limited to environmental taxes. In one area after another – health care, housing, retirement planning – tax policy intersects with nontax problems. Indeed, one of the defining features of American tax culture is the use of tax policy to solve problems that are addressed elsewhere by direct government spending. The mortgage interest deduction, the treatment of qualified pension plans, and the taxes that accompanied the Affordable Care Act ("Obamacare") are examples of this phenomenon. Each of these areas involves a mixture of tax policy (fairness, efficiency, simplicity) and nontax policy (homeowners versus renters, single versus multiple payors) issues, to the point where it is frequently impossible to distinguish between the two. The same is true at the state level, where alcohol and cigarette taxes confront problems of regressivity and externalities not entirely dissimilar from a carbon levy. That the federal government has not imposed a carbon tax, while individual states have at least considered doing so, is likewise typical of the US federal system, in which state and local governments frequently experiment in areas where there is no national consensus. From this perspective, environmental taxes are simply a more extreme version of an old problem, involving an inseparable mix of tax and nontax issues and requiring a sensitivity to different subcultures and political institutions in order to achieve success.

Will environmental taxes eventually become more similar, or will they continue to drift apart? In theory they should present a good candidate for convergence. Since everyone breathes the same air, environmental taxes would appear to resemble cross-border tax provisions more than (say) family tax or similar issues that have a primarily local impact. The multilateral approach to environmental issues, as in the Kyoto and Paris agreements, suggests a coordination of policy not usually present in tax matters.[46] But even these agreements typically state overall goals and leave individual countries free to decide what methods (taxes, regulation, cap and trade, and so forth) will be employed to achieve them, leaving rather wide latitude for implementation.[47] It is instructive, in this vein, that even the EU has had limited success in coordinating environmental taxes, with the Nordic countries in particular taking a very different approach from their European neighbors. The pattern that we observed in earlier chapters, of convergence at a broad but superficial level coupled

46 President Trump announced the United States would withdrawal from Kyoto in 2017.

47 A process calling to mind Jonathan Wiener's distinction between "horizontal" and "vertical" borrowing in environmental law, generally. Jonathan B. Wiener, "Something Borrowed for Something Blue: Legal Transplants and the Evolution of Global Environmental Law," *Ecology Law Quarterly*, 27 (2001), 1295–1372.

with continued and even growing divergence in the details of policy and administration, would thus appear to be reasserting itself in the environmental tax area.

The bottom line would appear to be that environmental taxes differ from other taxes in degree but not necessarily in kind. In this and other areas countries face similar problems but respond to them in different ways, depending on a mix of attitudes, institutions, and historical or geographic factors. (Sweden would probably worry less about energy costs if it had Italy's weather.) Convergence is a slow and painful process and countries move apart as readily as they come together, in some cases more so. Issues are global but decisions are local, and achieving consensus requires a sensitivity to political and cultural differences in this area no less than others.

## 6.6 MORE ON TAX LIFE CYCLES: WILL CARBON TAXES SOMEDAY DISPLACE INCOME TAXES?

Although significant enough on their own terms, environmental taxes also suggest the issue of tax life cycles, referred to in the discussion of progressivity earlier in this chapter. Income is, in theory, inexhaustible: there will always be some new way to make money from the sale of goods, services, or other benefits. By contrast, carbon is a limited resource: someday, sooner or later, it will run out. The use of carbon-based fuels also has negative externalities, as discussed above, which have become more and more prominent in both political and economic discourse. Some people think that, left unchecked, global warming will eventually destroy the planet altogether, or at very least make human life impossible or unrecognizable in nature.

Given the above, would it make sense for a carbon tax to displace the income tax entirely, rather than merely supplementing it in a few countries, as is now the case? Will students one day take "Introduction to Carbon Taxation" as a basic law school course, with income and business entity taxes reduced to electives? Or might carbon and other environmental taxes come to replace the income tax in stages, the former being gradually adopted by one country after another, and the latter being subject to more and more exemptions, deductions, and credits until it eventually became a shadow of its former self, like the American estate tax and federal excise taxes today?

The suggestion seems fanciful now, but it may be less so in the future. The attrition of the progressive income tax, especially when applied to capital as opposed to labor income, has already attracted worldwide attention. The carbon tax is at present limited to a small number of countries, but so was the income tax a hundred or so years ago. It is also noteworthy that the criticisms now leveled at carbon taxes – that they are elitist, politically unrealistic, and destructive of commercial activity – are not entirely different from the critiques of the early income tax. The regions that have adopted or at least considered carbon taxes, including the Nordic countries and some of the more progressive American states, have frequently been a decade or two ahead of other geographic areas, although they too have guessed wrongly at times. Nontax efforts to reduce carbon consumption, by legislation or regulatory fiat, have proved difficult or impossible in many places, much as nontax efforts to deal with large concentrations of wealth proved difficult in the past.

The early income tax has sometimes been described as the convergence of a "push" – the need for new revenue on the part of modern welfare states, and a "pull" – the availability of large, highly publicized incomes as a potential revenue source. Might the same thing happen sooner or later with carbon taxes, beginning in a few jurisdictions and spreading out from them? Does the adoption of carbon taxes in Sweden and neighboring countries constitute a first step in this direction?

The suggestion above will likely remain an outlier for the foreseeable future. But it demonstrates the value of studying different tax cultures and the insights, both theoretical and practical, which can be gleaned from pursuing such a study. The boundary between tax and other subjects is highly porous, and the study of comparative tax law may at times be more interesting and productive than an exclusive focus on one's own native country. Looking outside of one's own garden is sometimes the best way of understanding what is going on within it, both today and in the future.

## 6.7 TAX TRANSPLANTS AND INTERNATIONAL ORGANIZATIONS: A NOTE ON "VERTICAL BORROWING"

Throughout this chapter we have generally assumed that transplants or borrowing were voluntary in nature, with tax systems converging, if at all, only because they wanted to do so. This is obviously not always the case. There may be an element of compulsion in the borrowing process, either overt in the case of international organizations or covert in the form of unequal bargaining power in the negotiation of tax treaties and similar bilateral arrangements. For example, the United States has exerted strong pressure on other countries to adopt the FACTA reporting standards and has frequently been aggressive in negotiations of other provisions as well, particularly in the area of business and investment taxes.[48] International Monetary Fund pressure on developing countries might also be placed in this category. This is before one even reaches colonialism or outright occupation of other countries, as in the case of Germany and Japan.

Writing in the area of environmental law, Jonathan Wiener has referred to the spread of rules in this manner as "vertical" rather than the more typical "horizontal" borrowing process, noting that this process may not always take adequate notice of the interest and potential of weaker, less developed countries.[49] Whether to call

48 See Chapter 4.
49 Wiener, "Something Borrowed," 1294, 1362–65.

these transplants or impositions is an open question, but unquestionably they play a significant role.

As noted above – and with the possible exception of the EU – international organizations play a lesser role in the tax field than in other areas of law. Thus, for the time being, it is reasonable to assume that most tax convergence will continue to take place as part of a voluntary, or partly voluntary, process. With the passage of time this may change, and the tax field may come to resemble (say) the environmental or trade areas more than it does right now. The discussion above suggests that this will be a slow and halting process.

## 6.8 WHAT DOESN'T CONVERGE: FAMILY TAX AND THE "TAX AND" PROBLEM

A common problem with studying taxation is that it can be difficult to separate from other areas of law. We have previously observed this problem in environmental taxation and, to a lesser extent, the tax avoidance issue. In some cases the issue is even more prominent.

A good example is the problem of family taxation. Should taxes be imposed on individuals or on the family unit? If the latter, how should the family be defined: married couples, married couples and their young or adult children, etc.? What about same-sex couples, unmarried heterosexuals, and other fact patterns that differ from traditional norms? What of divorces, prenuptial agreements, and transfers to spouses, children, or other relatives? Should the answer to these questions be determined on the basis of value-neutral criteria – if there indeed is such a thing in this area – or does the state have a right to promote lifestyles it approves of and punish those it dislikes? Finally, how should these questions be resolved: at the legislative, administrative, or judicial level or (failing this) on an individual, case-by-case basis?

The issues above are all tax questions, but not only that. They are closely tied to family law and policy which, in turn, reflects deeply held values in individual countries. Such issues – which are of extreme importance to the overall progressivity and impact of the income tax – are also less likely to be scrutinized at the international level, although they do come up frequently in tax treaties.

Given the above, it is not surprising that there is less convergence in family tax issues than (say) tax rates or tax avoidance, perhaps even less than environmental taxes. Thus, the United States has joint returns for married couples, which are unheard of and even unconstitutional in some European countries.[50] The Internal Revenue Code allows a deduction for alimony payments and counts them in the recipient's income: again, the opposite of the practice in most nations. This is before

[50] The unconstitutionality results from the requirement to consider an individual's taxpaying capacity, and not that of their spouse, in the taxing process. This issue was discussed briefly in Chapter 5.

one even reaches concepts like the Hindu Undivided Family, a filing option in India that would be quite extraordinary in other jurisdictions. To some extent, these differences result from the reduced scrutiny afforded individual taxes – not enough people move from India to the United States in a given year to make it a hot political issue – but they also reflect religious and cultural values that are more difficult to compromise on than the rules for affiliated groups or consolidated returns. To put the matter differently, tax law reflects the pattern in comparative law generally: a higher degree of convergence for provisions that affect international business or capital flows and a rather lower level for those that don't, at least not in a direct fashion.

Is family tax an outlier or a matter of degree? A powerful strand of family law scholarship suggests that it may be the former. Going by the name of family law exceptionalism, this scholarship argues that family law has been purposefully excluded from the comparative law mainstream in order to maintain the broader distinction between family and market and, with it, the subjugation of women on an economic, social, and political plane.[51] Following this analysis, the notion of comparative law as inherently private, traditional, and national in character – a separate field and subject to separate rules – is itself part of this ongoing project.[52]

Does the concept of exceptionalism also apply in the tax area? The idea is far from ridiculous. Most tax scholars are male, and tax scholarship has historically emphasized business and investment taxation. Comparative tax scholarship has if anything been even more diffident. From this perspective, the relatively slow convergence of family tax rules may be a matter of choice rather than something inevitable.

Yet from a broader perspective, the differences between family and business taxation appear to be a matter of degree rather than kind. Issues like progressive taxation or tax avoidance also involve cultural clashes, although their role is somewhat less obvious in these areas. Even subjects as mundane as housing taxation or the distinction between business and personal expenses reflect cultural choices.[53] In any event, there is no clear line between family and other issues: Italian tax progressivity is undercut by the resistance to joint returns, and tax-free transfers to spouses are central to US estate planning. Indeed, the choice of taxable unit – individual, family, or a hybrid of the two – is both logically and temporally precedent to these other issues.

Rather than rules and exceptions, it seems more accurate to say that there is a continuum between tax issues, which display a higher or lower degree of convergence based on the nature of the associated values, degree of financial

51 See, e.g., Janet Halley & Kerry Rittich, "Critical Directions in Comparative Family Law: Genealogies and Contemporary Studies of Family Exceptionalism: Introduction to the Special Issue on Comparative Family Law," *American Journal of Comparative Law*, 58 (2010), 754.

52 See generally Frances E. Olsen, "The Family and the Market: A Study of Ideology and Legal Reform," *Harvard Law Review* 96 (7) (1983), 1497–1578.

53 See generally Anthony C. Infanti & Bridget Crawford, *Critical Tax Theory: An Introduction* (Cambridge University Press, 2009).

pressure, and other factors. In this sense, tax is not fundamentally different from other areas of law, but perhaps a little bit ahead of the curve, the rapid movement of money and individuals meaning that differences in tax law attract attention somewhat earlier than those in other areas. Rather than being a step behind, tax may yet find itself just a little bit ahead of its intellectual competitors.

## 6.9 EXAMINING THE EVIDENCE: CONVERGENCE, DIVERGENCE, AND THE ENDURING PROBLEM OF CULTURE

Examining our case studies we see similarities but also differences. The progressive income tax applies in all but a handful of countries, but its effective as opposed to nominal progressivity varies substantially. All countries are officially opposed to tax avoidance, but their enforcement tools and the enthusiasm with which they approach the subject remain quite different. Environmental taxes have proved attractive in some places but not in others, provoking a debate that mixes tax and environmental policy considerations in a manner similar to health care and other issues. Family tax appears to converge more slowly than other areas, but whether this results from choice or necessity remains somewhat unclear. In at least some of these areas individual countries appear to be diverging rather than converging, especially when the substance as opposed to the form of their tax systems is taken into account. At times both phenomena occur simultaneously, a superficial convergence masking an equal or greater difference in day-to-day results. Even identical rules take on new meanings in a different national context.

A case study approach thus confirms the conclusions of previous chapters but fills in some important details. Culture remains important, and convergence comes slowly if at all in most areas. But the pressure for convergence, and the significance of culture in resisting it, varies significantly between policy areas. Convergence is greater with respect to tax rates than tax bases; with respect to the need to prevent tax avoidance than the actual methods employed to combat it; with respect to broad, generic environmental goals than specific environmental (and especially environmental tax) strategies. All countries seek fairness, simplicity, and economic efficiency in the same sense that all countries seek peace, freedom, and justice: but these terms mean different things to different people. Tax rules and principles are frequently difficult to separate from more general, preexisting legal norms, which are themselves difficult to separate from a country's underlying history, politics, culture, and institutional structure. Countries are subject to varying pressures depending on their size, wealth, and geographic location. Individual countries import some tax norms and export others at the same time.

None of the above should be especially surprising, except perhaps to those who spend too much time at international tax conferences, or have become just a little bit too enthusiastic about the globalization phenomenon. It is, at bottom, merely another way of saying that comparative tax is one part of the larger phenomenon of comparative law, and subject to the same limitations that apply in these areas.[54] The assumption that tax will be different reflects either an excessive pride in the field or (more likely) a large-scale ignorance of the others: it does not survive an in-depth study of actual practice in different areas of tax law and in different national contexts.

More surprising than the convergence/divergence dichotomy are the factors that appear to explain it. One would think intuitively that convergence would be less likely when countries are separated by deeply held values and attitudes, which are difficult to change, and more likely when they are distinguished by institutional or historical differences, which (one would think) could be adjusted without unnecessary harm. The very concept of national character – traditionally conceived as a set of values and attitudes rather than mere institutional difference – suggests that this will be the case.

Yet experience suggests that the opposite is often true. Differences in tax progressivity and antiavoidance strategies result at least as much from legislative and judicial structures as from popular values and attitudes. Environmental taxes depend to a very substantial extent upon political precedent, the level of confidence placed in the tax administration, and geographic quirks: it cannot be said that countries enacting such taxes are necessarily more concerned about the environment than those which do not. Even family tax, the most obviously value-laden of the areas studied, depends on a mixture of attitudes, institutions, and historical factors: it is an "outlier" only in the sense that these factors balance out differently than in other areas. This is similar to the pattern observed in nontax law and described in our previous chapters.[55] Anyone who believes that these differences can be eliminated merely by tinkering with existing institutional arrangements – or by additional pressure from international organizations – is likely to be disappointed.

There is, to be sure, a great deal of borrowing or transplanting in the tax area. The 1986 US tax reform unquestionably precipitated similar reforms in other countries, even if they were to some degree superficial in nature. Nordic environmental taxes provide a model for other European and non-European countries and even for some North American states and provinces, although there has been significant political resistance as well.[56] The war against tax avoidance requires substantial cooperation and coordination with respect to information gathering, taxpayer auditing, and substantive legal provisions. Even family taxation is not wholly immune to the imitation and borrowing phenomenon. The growth of China as a tax power may

54 See Chapter 1.

55 In my comparative law course, students frequently observe that differences between (say) American and French judicial opinions have at least as much to do with institutional differences as with the supposed "national character" of France and the United States. For example, French opinions tend to list statutes and conclusions without much explanation of their underlying logic. This may be termed "French" in a broad philosophical sense but has little to do with the attitudes of average Frenchmen.

56 One observer has described the Nordic countries as "norm entrepreneurs" in this and other areas. See Christine Ingebritsen, *Scandinavia's Role in World Politics* (Lanham: Rowman & Littlefield, 2006).

eventually exert a gravitational pull not entirely different from the United States and its allies in our generation. As time passes, it seems likely that this sort of convergence will continue to grow.

The discussion above has interesting implications for the role of international organizations in the tax field. From the perspective of transplant theory, international organizations may be understood as an effort to streamline the transplant and (eventually) the convergence process, either by compulsion as in the case of the EU, gentle persuasion in the case of the OECD and other cooperative organizations, or force of example in the case of academic exchanges and other educational programs. But these efforts have thus far met with only limited success, for reasons similar to those cited above. Indeed, the trend, to the extent there is one, appears to be away from convergence and toward the reassertion of separate national identities in law and other matters: part of the general reaction against globalism that has become a defining trend of our era. Populist movements in numerous countries are one but not the only example of this trend. The policies of both the United States and China – currently the two largest actors on the world stage – each reflect this development.

All this is before we reach the problem of superficial convergence or "surface law," that is, a country's pretending to adhere to an international norm and simply continuing sub rosa to do what it was doing before. One example of this might be the adoption of uniform tax rates that are subject to so many exceptions as to be largely ineffective. Another example might be the adoption of a highly publicized program against tax shelters that is then only loosely enforced, if at all. This sort of thing is common in all areas of law, but the complexity and opaqueness of tax administration, together with the perceived need to make one's tax system appear recognizable to foreign investors, make it a particularly attractive strategy in the tax area. The willingness of most countries to agree to some version of the BEPS program, although one suspects that their actual policies will remain different, is a further example of this phenomenon.

The convergence problem takes us back to where we started: to the overall state of comparative taxation and its relationship, both theoretical and practical, to comparative law in general. If tax experts have at times lagged behind other scholars, developments in the field may actually be ahead of those in other areas of practice. This creates a challenge but also an opportunity for scholars who are able to break out of existing patterns. The following chapter considers this relationship and how it might better be approached in the future.

# 7

# Conclusion: The Limits of Globalization and the Continuing Importance of Culture

We began this book with a survey of the comparative tax field and its current limitations. We proceeded to construct a theoretical model of tax culture that included attitudes, institutions, and a not insignificant number of historical and geographic quirks or contingencies that are difficult to fit in any category. Armed with this background, we considered a number of contemporary issues, including the question of convergence in tax policy, the problem of non-Western countries, and (in Chapter 6) three specific policy areas, some of which appeared to be converging and some of which remained culturally bound. In the process, we reached several conclusions but left other questions unanswered, and perhaps even contradicted ourselves a few times along the way.

Where does this brief survey leave us?

Rather than reinventing the wheel (metaphorically speaking), it may be useful to state a few of our principal conclusions in summary form. This runs the risk of rewarding people who turn immediately to the last chapter, but such people will most surely be punished in the afterlife if not earlier, when they attempt the same method on novels and other nonfiction.[1] Following the above, we will state a few further unanswered questions and make the usual suggestions for additional research.

Here, then, are a few principal takeaways:

1. Although it is difficult to quantify, it remains possible to discuss tax culture in systematic terms. A comprehensive definition should include both tax attitudes – what average taxpayers and tax decision-makers think about tax issues – and tax institutions, that is, the legal, political, and economic structures that turn inchoate tax attitudes into actual tax policy results. For the sake of convenience, we have labeled the study of the former "tax anthropology" and of the latter "tax

[1] I once read *The Sun Also Rises* without realizing when and how the hero (Jake) was wounded. The professor was unimpressed.

sociology," but this is a rather arbitrary distinction, and both attitudes and institutions are properly part of the definition of culture in tax or any other field.

2. While laymen tend to use tax culture primarily to discuss attitudes, institutions are frequently more important in determining specific tax outcomes and in explaining the differences between different countries. Indeed, a third category, which we have labeled historical quirks or contingencies, is sometimes as or more important than the first two categories combined. This phenomenon is not limited to the tax field but is perhaps stronger here than elsewhere, because so many tax institutions were borrowed ("transplanted") from one country to another and have little if anything to do with current attitudes or existing nontax institutions in the country in question. While it might be assumed that institutions were easier to change than values, in practice the opposite is often true: once established, institutions are surprisingly difficult to change, even when they conflict with current reality or with behavior in other, similar nations. There is accordingly a high degree of inertia or "stickiness" in national tax policy that defies broader international trends and sometimes defies logic itself.
3. Because tax culture remains important, the convergence or standardization of tax law proceeds unevenly and in some cases not at all. When it does take place, the process of convergence is often superficial in nature, with countries adopting the same broad concepts but applying them in such different ways that they become unrecognizable in practice. The issues of tax progressivity, where countries often adopt similar tax rate schedules but use different definitions of income, and antiavoidance measures, which most countries have enacted but which they interpret with varying degrees of enthusiasm, are two prominent examples of this phenomenon. So-called carbon taxes, which involve varying perspectives on tax and environmental issues, provide a further example. Even when countries adopt similar rules, economic, cultural, and geographic differences suggest that the rules will have different practical effects: family taxes and environmental taxes are among the many examples of this problem.
4. Transnational institutions, like the EU or OECD, provide a significant counterbalance to the factors above, encouraging a convergence of institutions and attitudes and resulting in the creation of a nascent global tax culture. Pressure for convergence is also supplied by multinational corporations, who may simply refuse to do business in countries that do not adhere to minimum norms of fairness and transparency in their tax policy. But these pressures are highly uneven in nature, being most significant for business tax issues and much less so for rules affecting individual taxpayers and their families. The pressures may also offset one another, transnational institutions being primarily concerned with correct or "good" tax policy and corporations typically seeking the lowest tax rates. Their significance as a counterweight to national tax cultures may thus be somewhat limited. Educational programs, like the NYU or Harvard LL.M., contribute to a sense of global tax culture among tax professionals, but it is

unclear how deeply this culture descends, and those educated in these programs face countervailing pressures when they return back home.

5. The rise of China, India, and other non-Western countries significantly complicates the issue of tax culture, because these countries have different attitudes and institutions and are likely to resist imposition of a global (read Western) cultural norm. While in the past the major Western powers could largely export their tax systems to other countries, these countries are simply too big and self-confident to let this happen. For China especially, the possibility of forcing other countries to adhere to Chinese norms, rather than vice-versa, is especially attractive. Russia, Japan, Brazil, and various Islamic countries present a lesser but similar challenge to Western preeminence: for example, the concept of tax progressivity and redistribution has a negative connotation in the former Eastern Bloc countries, which stands a significant portion of traditional tax policy more or less on its head.
6. The combination of items 1 to 5 above suggests a profound skepticism regarding the globalization phenomenon in tax law and, perhaps, in law more generally. Stated differently, national tax cultures remain highly distinct and there is little indication of their becoming less so with the passage of time. If there is a globalization process, it remains highly uneven, depending upon the area of law in question; the size and location of the relevant country; and the level of decision-making (regional, national, or local) that is involved. While in some ways globalization is more advanced in tax than in other fields, in other ways it is slower: the sense of taxation as a key component of sovereignty, and its implication of basic cultural values (fairness, equality, etc.), serve as important counterweights to the rise of global markets and the relatively free flow of tax ideas between countries. This too is unlikely to change in the near future.
7. Although a global tax culture is slow to appear, an awareness of culture may be of significant benefit in assessing national tax systems. By studying culture in a systematic way, scholars gain important insights into the success or failure of specific tax policies and the degree to which these policies are, or are not, transferable to other nations and regions. For example, the Scandinavian system of relatively high taxes and welfare payments may be appealing to progressives in other countries, but it is difficult to separate from other aspects of Nordic tax culture (high degree of compliance, efficient and largely electronic tax administration, and so forth) that may be more difficult to transport. Western concepts of tax policy may likewise take on a different significance in postcommunist or developing world societies. International organizations like the IMF or OECD, together with university tax programs, are likely to be more effective if they learn to respect cultural differences rather than merely exporting what amounts to an essentially Anglo-American worldview. Each of these conclusions would likely be true for other areas of law, but it is easy to forget them in the tax field, with its frequent assumption of universal values and universally applicable models and

(what is closely related) its inherited tendency to condescend to smaller nations and non-Western values. A major purpose of this book is to argue for cultural sensitivity and thus to the degree possible reverse these tendencies.

The items above constitute the principal conclusions of this study, but numerous questions remain for future scholars. Here, in similarly barebones form, are a few of the more important ones:

A. There is need for vastly more work on the tax cultures of individual countries, particularly institutional/historical aspects. The work of Sven Steinmo on Sweden, the United Kingdom, and the United States suggests how valuable such research can be. The work of Jinyan Li and others in China is potentially of similar import (I am not aware of a parallel study on India at this point.) This is time-consuming work, and probably best attempted after one has tenure and a substantial research budget, but it is invaluable if we are to move beyond superficial description. The work is best undertaken by someone who knows the language and culture of the country in question, but that may be less of a barrier than commonly thought: growing up in India doesn't mean that you know anything much about Indian taxes, and a foreigner with an open mind and a laptop can probably catch up quickly.

B. Together with work on individual countries there is also a need for further comparative studies of specific tax issues. This includes broad areas like business or family taxation but also more specific subjects like environmental taxes, antiabuse rules, or the details of tax enforcement and administration. As in any social science, comprehensive and detailed studies of a particular issue tend to be more productive than broad-brush descriptions. To be effective, these studies should include assessments of the real-world impact of tax rules rather than a simple comparison of law as written in statute books.

C. There is room for much more work on international organizations, including those exercising "hard" power (like the EU or perhaps the IMF) and those with primarily "softer" influence (like the Harvard or NYU international tax programs). The work of Ruth Mason and Alison Christians is an example of what can be done in this area. The challenge here is less one of language than of perspective: to study international organizations effectively, one must learn to cultivate a reporter's skepticism regarding the goals and effectiveness of a system of which one is oneself a part. A critical assessment of tax graduate programs – what do they actually teach and what do the students actually take home with them – would be especially valuable.

D. There is a pressing need for more interdisciplinary work involving tax and other legal scholars and – perhaps more important – anthropologists, sociologists, and other social scientists. There is some hypocrisy in saying this, since I wrote this book alone, and for the same reasons others do so: time, convenience, and the difficulty of finding common ground between the cultures (so to speak) of different academic disciplines. But without collaboration it is hard to move beyond an elementary understanding of what are essentially anthropological and sociological concepts. Writing a book about "culture" without an anthropology background is a little bit like predicting the deficit without professional economists, or self-diagnosing for a serious medical problem: people do it, but the results are often suboptimal.

E. The subject of tax transplants cries out for additional study, both on a theoretical level and with regard to individual issues. What are the factors that account for successful and unsuccessful tax transplants, and how do they differ from other areas of law? Does this success or failure depend on broader similarities or differences in tax cultures, or on more technical factors? The work of Carlo Garbarino and Jinyan Li represents an important beginning, but there is much more to be done. This is really another way of saying that comparative tax has to "catch up" with comparative law, and give more systematic thought to the borrowing/convergence phenomenon as it relates to real-world, practical issues.
F. A new research agenda should be complemented by changes in tax education, to make international and (especially) comparative tax the starting point for tax learning rather than an afterthought. This is already happening to some degree in LL.M. programs, but the change is much slower at the J.D. level. Even in LL.M. programs, my sense is that "international tax" tends to mean the taxation of cross-border transactions, with the comparative aspect – inevitably less profitable – as a sort of secondary item. I personally try to include a comparative tax element even in my basic tax course: many of the students don't get it, but that's also true when I teach deductions or fringe benefits in the US tax system, and at least I've got them moving in the right direction. One good strategy here is to pick out a single issue, like joint returns or the taxation of marriage and divorce, and see how a few countries approach it: you don't need much tax background to understand these issues, and they provide a useful window into larger political and cultural differences. One can also begin with a comparison between different state taxes and segue from that into the tax systems of foreign countries. (There is no real difference between multistate and multinational taxation, except that the South lost the Civil War, so the federal government is stronger than (say) the EU. The underlying issues are the same.)

The suggestions above pertain primarily to the tax field. But they suggest the need to change the culture – that word again – of the legal academy more generally. If I may be permitted one final list, these changes would include the following:

i. There is a need for more empiricism and less normativity in all areas of legal scholarship, and not merely the tax field. This should also involve greater respect for collaborative work with nonlawyers who may provide the empirical skills that some legal scholars lack. (The work of Elizabeth Warren on bankruptcy is one example.) In no other academic field would empirical scholarship be considered inferior to normative argument that proposes solutions to obscure problems, frequently of more interest to the author than the reader, and typically without very much scientific basis for doing so. Empirical work is an acquired taste for many law professors, because it means at least temporarily leaving the ivory tower and confronting what actually happens in the real world. But if you're describing an imaginary world, why would anyone be interested in your ideas in the first place?

ii. The definition of empiricism should be expanded beyond number-crunching to include systematic but nonquantifiable description of legal phenomena that the reader is not otherwise familiar with. Empirical is not the same as quantitative. Nor is description, or mere description, a four-letter word. Whether or not we follow Clifford Geertz and demand "thick description" of Balinese cockfights, observation and description of legal phenomena has a value in itself and is a prerequisite for normative arguments. This is especially true for comparative law, where basic knowledge of relevant facts is often unavailable without academic work.

iii. Legal teaching as well as scholarship should reflect a greater emphasis on empiricism – what used to be called "fact-finding" – and a less exclusive emphasis on normative argument. One of the basic characteristics of the common law system is its emphasis on "facts to law" as opposed to, or together with, "law to facts" reasoning.[2] Yet the traditional law school curriculum is heavily focused on appellate judicial decisions and may leave students with relatively limited skills at independent fact-gathering. Clinical programs have somewhat changed this balance, including both real-world clinics and law school simulation courses, like business planning or small business counseling. (Tax assistance programs, which emphasize basic tasks like ascertaining the taxpayer's income and the number of dependents if any, provide a further example.) But these skills have, in most cases, yet to be integrated into the mainstream curriculum. Hiring professors with more real-world experience would be one important step in this direction.

iv. Recommendations D and E from the preceding list, regarding interdisciplinary research and the study of legal transplants, should be extended beyond the tax field, including comparative law and other subjects.

v. Likewise for recommendation E, regarding the incorporation of comparative issues in introductory law school courses, which is frequently talked about but rarely done in American law schools. (European universities may be a bit ahead on this score.) Even a small comparative unit in each introductory course would make a significant difference here.

[2] See Chapter 5.

## A CONCLUDING THOUGHT

The discussion above applies primarily to lawyers and law schools. But the study of culture may also help to redress a larger imbalance in Western society, one which goes well beyond the legal profession. This imbalance has intellectual but also political roots, involving the nature of expertise and the relationship between experts ("elites") and the general population. It is a problem that has been long in developing, but has become more urgent in recent years.

The past decade has witnessed a revolt, called populist by its proponents and authoritarian or even fascist by its opponents, against ruling elites in the United States and other countries. Although partly a matter of personalities, the revolt reflects a genuine perception that elites are out of touch with the general public both on specific issues and overall philosophy. The revolt has spread so far and so fast that some observers believe that our entire political system is "off the rails" and the rule of law itself is threatened in the United States and other countries.

One frequent criticism of Western elites is that they have become excessively comfortable with subjects that can be reduced to numbers, like economic statistics and election results, and insufficiently sensitive to things that are more difficult to quantify, like religion, nationalism, and personal happiness: in a word, culture. This imbalance sometimes expresses itself in frustration at behavior that the elites believe to be irrational but which, on further thought, reflects cultural differences. For example, some liberals believe that conservatives are irrational because they support policies that would hurt them economically, although the latter may have valid noneconomic (i.e., cultural) reasons for doing so. For their part, conservatives see liberal attachment to cultural values (gender equity, freedom of expression) as hypocritical or trivial in nature without considering the centrality of these values to the liberal worldview. This failure to take culture seriously has led some people to embrace an opposite extreme, in which they reject quantitative reasoning altogether and appear to be concerned only with their own instinctive viewpoint. (The refusal to accept overwhelming evidence regarding the existence of global warming is an extreme example of this phenomenon.) Behavior of this latter sort may at first appear to be the opposite of elite condescension, but it is the flip side of the same coin: i.e., the failure to take culture seriously, and to achieve a proper balance between thought and feeling in the making and carrying out of public policy.[3] A healthy society requires the existence of precisely that balance.

Only a fraction of Americans goes to law school. But it is a highly significant fraction. Lawyers play a disproportionate role in government, politics, and the framing of issues for public policy debate. When law students are taught that economics is important, but anthropology – the study of culture – is trivial, this belief carries over to their

[3] The failure is part of an idolization of numbers and statistics in society generally, and a concomitant dismissal of anything that cannot be quantified. Anyone who has recently watched a baseball game, or the Jeopardy television program, knows what I'm talking about.

professional and personal lives. When they learn that facts are something to be plugged into a predetermined argument, rather than considered on their own merits, this too carries over. Nor is the problem above limited to legal education: natural and some social scientists are if anything taught to be even more dismissive of culture than are lawyers, or at least (what amounts to essentially the same thing) of any culture except their own.

I should clarify that I am not calling for a sort of Luddite rejection of social science or the elevation of "culture," a notoriously squishy term, to an unassailable position. (A lot of very nasty things have been justified under the cultural label.) Nor do I think that cultural arguments should be immune from evaluation and criticism, for fear of giving offense or being considered insufficiently open-minded.

What I am calling for is rather an expansion of our intellectual consciousness, to realize that things that cannot be converted to numbers may still be enormously important in public affairs, and rightfully so. Were I living in eighteenth-century France, I would be staking out a position somewhere between Descartes, the logician, and Rousseau, who thought that the role of feeling should remain important even in a post-Enlightenment world.[4] The point is not to accept culture in an unthinking way, but to study it with the same energy, enthusiasm, and discipline that we study other important subjects. This is the real lesson of "deep description" as undertaken by Clifford Geertz and others: not that culture be unthinkingly accepted, but that it be evaluated in a systematic and persistent manner even though it cannot be reduced to a simple formula or series of formulas. As an interface between social science on the one hand, and day-to-day life on the other, lawyers are uniquely suited to undertake such studies and to attempt to redress the balance between thought and feeling in a workable, ongoing manner. Nobody else can do it for them.

Thirty years ago I attended a talk in which the speaker, a prominent legal philosopher, referred to American law schools as a "hierarchy of smart alecks."[5] One could say the same today about our entire society. The sense that only one kind of knowledge – rational, logical, and above all quantifiable – matters and everything else is more or less worthless plays an important role in maintaining this hierarchy. An appreciation of cultural differences will not necessarily make us wiser and cleverer than we were before. But it may teach us something else: a sense of humility and a recognition of our own limitations. Sometimes, that is the most important of all.

4 See generally Simon Blackburn, *The Oxford Dictionary of Philosophy* (3rd ed.) (Oxford University Press, 2016).

5 The speech was the basis for a book, which the author later updated. Roberto Mangabeira Unger. *The Critical Legal Studies Movement: Another Time, a Greater Task* (London & New York: Verso, 2015).

# Index

Printed in the United Kingdom by TJ Clays Ltd.